Revision

Framework

MATHS

National Curriculum Levels 3-5

David Capewell
Jayne Kranat
Peter Mullarkey

OXFORD
UNIVERSITY PRESS

OXFORD
UNIVERSITY PRESS

Great Clarendon Street, Oxford OX2 6DP

Oxford University Press is a department of the University of Oxford.
It furthers the University's objective of excellence in research,
scholarship, and education by publishing worldwide in

Oxford New York

Auckland Cape Town Dar es Salaam Hong Kong Karachi
Kuala Lumpur Madrid Melbourne Mexico City Nairobi
New Delhi Shanghai Taipei Tokyo Toronto

With offices in

Argentina Austria Brazil Chile Czech Republic France Greece
Guatemala Hungary Italy Japan South Korea Poland Portugal
Singapore Switzerland Thailand Turkey Ukraine Vietnam

British Library Cataloguing in Publication Data

Data available

ISBN 13 9780199149421
ISBN 019 914942 9

10 9 8 7 6 5 4 3 2

Typeset by Mathematical Composition Setters Ltd.

Printed by Unigraph, Spain.

Acknowledgements

The publisher would like to thank QCA for their kind permission to use
Key Stage 3 test questions.

About this book

This book has been written to help you revise for the National Tests at the end of KS3 Mathematics and is aimed at the 3–5 tier of entry.

The books consists of three types of pages:
▷ Contents pages that set out the information you need to know and provide practice
▷ Revision pages that consist of past paper test questions
▷ Practice test paper pages that provide confidence for the real thing.

The **Content** pages are organised into Number (N), Algebra (A), Shape, space and measure (S) and Data handling (D).

They tell you the main ideas you need to know and remember.

Key points tell you the information you need to know.

▶ A **prime number** has exactly two factors: 1 and itself.

> 1 is not a prime number – it only has one factor.

Worked examples show the skills you need in the tests, and margin boxes give you extra hints and tips.

example

If you are a years old now, how old will you be in 3 years time?
....
You will be $a + 3$ years old.

> **Check:**
> If you are 14 now, you'll be 17 in 3 years time:
> $a + 3 = 14 + 3 = 17$

The questions give you plenty of practice at specific National Curriculum levels so you can measure your progress against national standards.

L3 **M** 1 Give one prime number between 11 and 20.

2 a Find two different odd numbers that add to 10.
   b Find two different even numbers that add to 10.

▷ **M** shows a mental test question.

▷ means you can use a calculator.

The **Revision** pages are numbered **R1** to **R6**. These pages are full of past paper Test questions at each of the relevant levels so you experience the style of question you will see in the actual Tests. Each question refers you back to the relevant spread so you can go back over any content you need to practice further.

At the end to the book, there are two **Practice Test Papers** which mirror the style and content of the real thing. If you take these tests under exam conditions you will get a good idea of how you are performing. Do take into account that the actual tests are slightly faster as you can write on them.

All the **Answers** are at the back of the book so you can test yourself.

Contents

Contents

How to revise using this book

A good way to revise is to start with the Revision pages (**R1** to **R6**) to see what you know and what you need to practice.

Do each one in turn.

Each question refers you back to the content that you need to practice.

To revise a topic:
▶ Read the page through slowly and carefully.
▶ Make sure you understand each step of the worked examples.
▶ Make sure you understand the information in each key point.
▶ Work through the topic questions, as they will help you identify which sorts of questions may cause problems.
▶ Read through the topic again a few days later to help you remember.

Once you are confident you understand the key ideas, set aside an hour and test yourself using Practice Test Paper 1. You can see the equipment you'll need at the start of the test–make sure you have it all ready before you start.

Remember that in the actual test you'll be able to fill in the answers of the sheet so it will take less time. You could allow yourself an extra 15 minutes in the Practice Test Papers for all the copying and filling you need to do.

Talk to your teacher about any difficulties you have found, then move on to Practice Test Paper 2.

Good luck!

▶ The position of each digit in a number decides its place value.

This is four thousand five hundred and sixty-one:

millions	hundred thousands	ten thousands	thousands	hundreds	tens	units
1 000 000	100 000	10 000	1000	100	10	1
			4	5	6	1

example

Write the number 54 321 in words.

....

Fifty-four thousand, three hundred and twenty-one.

ten thousands	thousands	hundreds	tens	units
5	4	3	2	1

▶ A decimal number has a whole number part and a decimal part.

This is thirty-four point seven nine one:

tens 10	units 1	.	tenths $\frac{1}{10}$	hundredths $\frac{1}{100}$	thousandths $\frac{1}{1000}$
3	4	.	7	9	1

You can use a place value table to help add and subtract decimals.

example

a   Add 0.1 to 4.58   **b**   Subtract 0.1 from 9.23

....

a
```
        units  .  tenths  hundredths
          4    .    5         8
    +     0    .    1
        ─────────────────────────
          4    .    6         8
```

b
```
        units  .  tenths  hundredths
          9    .    2         3
    −     0    .    1
        ─────────────────────────
          9    .    1         3
```

You can write money using decimals:

▷   £3.45 is three pounds and forty-five pence
▷   £6.05 is six pounds and five pence
▷   £0.38 is thirty-eight pence

£6.50 is 6 pounds fifty pence.

When you multiply or divide by 10, 100 or 1000 the digits stay in the same order:

Multiply by 10:
▶ the digits move 1 place to the left. $123 \times 10 = 1230$

Multiply by 100:
▶ the digits move 2 places to the left. $123 \times 100 = 12\ 300$

Multiply by 1000:
▶ the digits move 3 places to the left. $123 \times 1000 = 123\ 000$

When you ×10, ×100, ×1000 expect a bigger answer.

Divide by 10:
▶ the digits move 1 place to the right. $123 \div 10 = 12.3$

Divide by 100:
▶ the digits move 2 places to the right. $123 \div 100 = 1.23$

Divide by 1000:
▶ the digits move 3 places to the right. $123 \div 1000 = 0.123$

When you ÷10, ÷100, ÷1000 expect a smaller answer.

Exercise N1

  1 Write in figures the number five hundred and six.

2 Write down the numbers in figures:

  a four hundred and twenty-eight
  b four hundred and one
  c one thousand and twenty-one

3 Write these numbers in words:

  a 247   **b** 1300   **c** 906

 4 What does the 8 represent in 45.8?

5 Sundeep throws the dice three times.
She arranges the scores to make 361.

  a What is the smallest number she can make using 3, 6 and 1?
  b What is the biggest number she can make using 3, 6 and 1?
  c What number is ten times bigger than 613?

6 Write what the 7 represents in each number:

  a 736   **b** 47.2   **c** 3.75

7 Write these numbers in figures:

  a thirty-four thousand, three hundred and seven
  b four hundred thousand and six
  c eighty-five point one two

8 Write these numbers in words:

  a 42 385   **b** 906 000   **c** 1 000 000

9 Calculate these:

  a $3.4 - 0.1$ **b** $3 - 0.1$ **c** $3.25 - 0.1$

 10 You are given these cards.
You don't have to use all the cards.

  a Write down the smallest number you can make.
  b Write down the largest number you can make.

  Use the cards to work out :
  c 5.6×10
  d 5.6×100
  e $5.6 \div 10$
  f $5.6 \div 100$

11 Divide 45 by 100. Give your answer as a decimal.

12 Work out:
  a $3.34 + 0.1$ **b** $45 + 0.1$
  c $3.6 + 0.01$ **d** $4.25 + 0.1$
  e $8.1 - 0.1$ **f** $3.24 - 0.01$

13 Write the missing number in these statements:
  a _____ $\times 100 = 423$
  b _____ $\times\ 10 = 8.6$
  c _____ $\div 100 = 0.4$

You can represent a number on a **number line**.

This is 47:

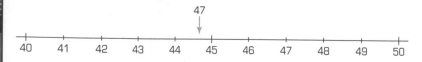

KEYWORDS
Order   Round
Number line

This is 3.54:

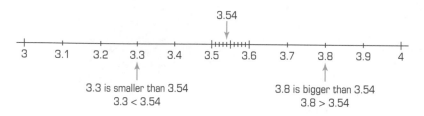

3.3 is smaller than 3.54
3.3 < 3.54

3.8 is bigger than 3.54
3.8 > 3.54

> means greater than
< means less than

You **order** numbers by arranging them in order of size.

example

Order these numbers from smallest to largest:
8.25   8.2   8.02   8.253   8.26

You can use a place value table.

10	1	•	$\frac{1}{10}$	$\frac{1}{100}$	$\frac{1}{1000}$
	8	•	2	5	0
	8	•	2	0	0
	8	•	0	2	0
	8	•	2	5	3
	8	•	2	6	0

On a number line:

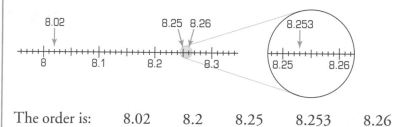

The order is: 8.02   8.2   8.25   8.253   8.26

See N1 for place value.

Position the numbers in the table so the decimal points are in a vertical line.

You can fill in the blank decimal places with 0s.

You can **round** a number to the nearest 1000, 100, 10, 1 or $\frac{1}{10}$.
▶ When a number is exactly halfway you round up.

example

a Round 78 to the nearest 10.

a 78 is between 70 and 80.
  It is 80 to the nearest 10.

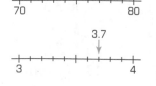

b Round 3.7 to the nearest whole number.

b 3.7 is between 3 and 4.
  It is 4 to the nearest whole number.

c Round 3.85 to one decimal place.

c 3.85 is halfway between 3.8 and 3.9.
  It is 3.9 to one decimal place.

Exercise N2

 M 1 The cost of a DVD is £8.95.
How much is this to the nearest pound?

2 What numbers are the arrows pointing to?

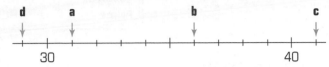

3 Order these numbers from smallest to largest.

a 36, 18, 23, 10, 6
b 76, 67, 676, 767, 667
c 1000, 990, 999, 1100, 1010

 M 4 The attendance at a football match is 23 631.
What is this to the nearest thousand?

5 What numbers are the arrows pointing to?

6 Order these numbers from smallest to largest.

a 3.8, 3.3, 2.8, 3.9, 3
b 9.5, 10.5, 10, 9, 10.1
c 3.5, 3.46, 3.55, 3.4, 3.6

 7 Find the number that is halfway between:

a 3 and 4   b 3.4 and 3.5   c 3 and 3.1

8 These are some record weights for vegetables.

Round each weight:
a to the nearest whole number
b to one decimal place.

Vegetable weight	
Potato	3.2 kg
Carrot	4.65 kg
Cabbage	56.24 kg

9 Use these number cards to make:

a the smallest possible number
b the largest possible number.

4	2	6	8

c Round your answers to a and b to the nearest 1000.

 M 10 Write down any number in between 3 and 3.1.
Do not write 3 or 3.1.

11 Use the correct inequality signs (> or <) between each pair of numbers:

a 8   8.5   b 3.5   3.4   c 2.1   1.9   d 3.52   3.51   e 3.46   3.5

12 What numbers are the arrows pointing to?

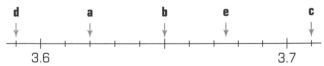

Whole numbers are **odd** or even.

1   2   3   4   5   6   7   8

▶ A **factor** is a number that divides into another number exactly.

example

Find the factors of 24.

$1 \times 24 = 24$ $2 \times 12 = 24$ $3 \times 8 = 24$ $4 \times 6 = 24$

The factors are 1, 2, 3, 4, 6, 8, 12, 24.

Imagine 24 dots arranged as rectangles, for example,

$3 \times 8 = 24$

These tests will help you decide whether a number is a factor:

Factor	2	3	4	5
Test	Number ends in 0, 2, 4, 6, 8	Sum of the digits divides by 3	Last two digits divide by 4	Number ends in 0 or 5

Factor	6	8	9	10
Test	Divides by both 2 and 3	Half the number divides by 4	Sum of the digits divides by 9	Number ends in 0

261 divides by 3 and 9 because:
$2 + 6 + 1 = 9$

example

Which of these numbers are in the 3 times table:
50   51   52   53   54   55

Add the digits. Does the sum divide by 3?

$50 \rightarrow 5 + 0 = 5$ $53 \rightarrow 5 + 3 = 8$

$51 \rightarrow 5 + 1 = ⑥$ $54 \rightarrow 5 + 4 = ⑨$

$52 \rightarrow 5 + 2 = 7$ $55 \rightarrow 5 + 5 = 10$

51 and 54 are in the 3 times table.

▶ A **prime number** has exactly two factors: 1 and itself.

1 is not a prime number – it only has one factor.

example

Is 8 a prime number?

$1 \times 8 = 8$ and $2 \times 4 = 8$ so 8 is not a prime number.

The prime numbers less than 20 are 2, 3, 5, 7, 11, 13, 17, 19.

▶ You multiply a number by a whole number to get a **multiple**.

The multiples of 4 are the same as the 4 times table: 4, 8, 12, 16, 20, ...

example

a Find the lowest common multiple (LCM) of 9 and 12.

b Find the highest common factor (HCF) of 16 and 24.

a List the multiples.
   9: 9, 18, 27, ㉟, 45, ...
   12: 12, 24, ㉟, 48, 60, ...
   36 is the lowest common multiple.

b List the factors.
   16: 1, 2, 4, ⑧, 16
   24: 1, 2, 3, 4, 6, ⑧, 12, 24
   8 is the highest common factor.

Exercise N3

L3 [M] **1** Give one prime number between 11 and 20.

2 a Find two different odd numbers that add to 10.
  b Find two different even numbers that add to 10.

3 a Arrange 10 dots into two different rectangles to draw the
    four factors of 10.
  b Arrange 7 dots into one rectangle to draw the factors of 7.
    What sort of number is 7?

4 Drinks can be bought in a 4-pack or a 6-pack.
  I buy exactly 20 drinks in the same sort of pack.
  Which sort of pack did I buy and how many did I buy?

L4 [M] **5** Write a factor of 80 which is between 10 and 20.

[M] **6** Write the first number after 100 that can be divided by 4.

[calculator] **7 a** Find the six factors of 32.
  b Find the nine factors of 36.

8 The year 2004 is a leap year as 2004 is divisible by 4.
  Check whether these are leap years:

  a 2012   **b** 2032   **c** 2018   **d** 2050

9 Copy the table and follow these instructions to
  discover 25 prime numbers.

  a Cross out the number 1.
  b Circle 2 and cross out all other multiples of 2.
  c Circle 3 and cross out all other multiples of 3.
  d Circle 5 and cross out all other multiples of 5.
  e Circle 7 and cross out all other multiples of 7.
  f Circle 11, 13 and any other number still left.
  g List the circled numbers.

1	2	3	4	5	6	7	8	9	10
11	12	13	14	15	16	17	18	19	20
21	22	23	24	25	26	27	28	29	30
31	32	33	34	35	36	37	38	39	40
41	42	43	44	45	46	47	48	49	50
51	52	53	54	55	56	57	58	59	60
61	62	63	64	65	66	67	68	69	70
71	72	73	74	75	76	77	78	79	80
81	82	83	84	85	86	87	88	89	90
91	92	93	94	95	96	97	98	99	100

10 a Pick an even number. Draw it as an arrangement of two rows of dots.
  b Pick an odd number. Draw it as an arrangement of two rows of dots.
  c When two even numbers or two odd numbers are added
    together, the answer is always even.
    Use your diagrams to explain why this happens.

L5 [M] **11** Write the first number after 100 that is divisible by 6.

[M] **12** Write a number that is less than 10 and has exactly three factors.

13 a Write the multiples of 8 from 8 to 96.
  b Write the multiples of 6 from 6 to 96.
  c What is the lowest common multiple of 6 and 8?

14 a Write the six factors of 20.
  b Write the six factors of 50.
  c What is the highest common factor of 20 and 50?

 15 There are three different buses that stop at a bus stop.
  Apple Buses stop every 2 minutes.
  Banana Buses stop every 3 minutes.
  Citrus Buses stop every 4 minutes.
  All three buses arrive at the same time.
  How long will it be before they all arrive at the same time again?

Triangular numbers can be arranged in triangles:

1   3   6   10

Square numbers can be arranged in squares:

1   4   9   16
(1 × 1)   (2 × 2)   (3 × 3)   (4 × 4)

A square number has an odd number of factors.
For example, 16 has five factors: 1, 2, 4, 8 and 16.

You can write square numbers using **powers**:

$1^2 = 1 \times 1 = 1$ $2^2 = 2 \times 2 = 4$ $3^2 = 3 \times 3 = 9$ $4^2 = 4 \times 4 = 16$

▶ The **square root** of a number multiplied by itself makes the number:
$3 \times 3 = 9$ so 3 is the square root of 9.

You write $\sqrt{9} = 3$.
$\sqrt{}$ means square root.

You can extend the number line to include **negative numbers**.

negative numbers   positive numbers

$^-6$ $^-5$ $^-4$ $^-3$ $^-2$ $^-1$ 0 1 2 3 4 5 6

$^-5$ < $^-3$ $^-1$ < 1   3 < 5

Positive numbers are greater than 0.
Negative numbers are less than 0.

> means greater than
< means less than

example

Order these integers from smallest to largest.
6      $^-5$ 2   0 $^-3$ 4 $^-4$

Use the number line:

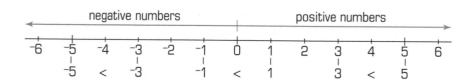

$^-5$ $^-4$ $^-3$ $^-2$ $^-1$ 0 1 2 3 4 5 6

$^-5$ $^-4$ $^-3$ 0   2   4   6

An integer is a positive or negative whole number, including zero.

You can use the number line to add and subtract integers.

example

Work out: **a** $^-3 + 5$ **b** $4 - 5$ **c** $^-2 - 3$.

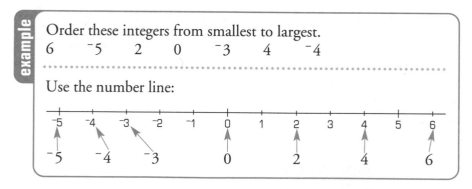

a Start at $^-3$ and move forwards 5:
$^-3 + 5 = 2$

+5
$^-5$ $^-4$ $^-3$ $^-2$ $^-1$ 0 1 2 3 4 5

b Start at 4 and move backwards 5:
$4 - 5 = {^-1}$

-5
$^-5$ $^-4$ $^-3$ $^-2$ $^-1$ 0 1 2 3 4 5

c Start at $^-2$ and move backwards 3:
$^-2 - 3 = {^-5}$

-3
$^-5$ $^-4$ $^-3$ $^-2$ $^-1$ 0 1 2 3 4 5

Exercise N4

1 What is 8 multiplied by 8?

2 Read the values of **a**, **b** and **c**.

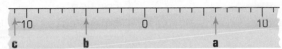

3 Order these temperatures from coldest to warmest.

8 °C   ⁻6 °C   3 °C   ⁻5 °C   0 °C

4 Choose the correct inequality sign (> or <) for these pairs of temperatures.

a 8 °C   5 °C   **b** 3 °C   1 °C   **c** ⁻3 °C   ⁻2 °C
d ⁻2 °C   1 °C   **e** 5 °C   5 °C

< means is less than

= means is equal to

> means is greater than

5 What is the square root of 16?

6 10 is the 4th triangular number.
What is the next triangular number?

7 a Write all the square numbers from 1 to 100.
b Write all the triangular numbers from 1 to 105.
c Write the two numbers that are both square and triangular.

8 Find the number that is halfway between ⁻3 and 5.

9 Find the new temperatures if a thermometer:

a starts at 8 °C, then drops by 13 °C
b starts at ⁻2 °C, then rises by 18 °C
c starts at ⁻1 °C, then drops by 3 °C

10 Put the correct sign (<, = or >) in each number sentence.

a 5 + 2   3 + 4
b 5 − 5   ⁻3
c 5   3 − 4
d ⁻2 − 3   ⁻6

< means is less than

= means is equal to

> means is greater than

11 Add six to minus three.

12 What number do you subtract from four to get minus 2?

13 Find the value of each of these.

a 18^2 **b** 1000^2 **c** $\sqrt{49}$ **d** $\sqrt{900}$

14 Complete this magic square.

15 a Find the total of these six numbers.

b Which three numbers add to give the smallest total?
What is this total?

▶ A fraction describes a part of a whole.

$\frac{1}{4}$ of this shape is blue:

KEYWORDS

| Fraction | Cancel |
| Equivalent | Equal |

1 part is blue ⟶ $\frac{1}{4}$
4 equal parts make the whole shape ⟶ $\frac{1}{4}$

You must divide the whole into equal parts.

example

Write down the fraction of each shape that is blue.

a   b   c

a $\frac{1}{2}$ b $\frac{2}{3}$ c $\frac{2}{5}$

▶ **Equivalent** fractions show the same amount.

Each diagram shows $\frac{1}{2}$ shaded.

$\frac{1}{2} = \frac{2}{4} = \frac{3}{6}$

$\frac{1}{2}$ $\frac{2}{4}$ $\frac{3}{6}$

You can find equivalent fractions by multiplying or dividing.

example

Cancel these fractions to their lowest form.

a $\frac{12}{18}$ b $\frac{9}{12}$ c $\frac{50}{100}$

a $\frac{12}{18} \overset{\div 6}{\underset{\div 6}{=}} \frac{2}{3}$ b $\frac{9}{12} \overset{\div 3}{\underset{\div 3}{=}} \frac{3}{4}$ c $\frac{50}{100} \overset{\div 50}{\underset{\div 50}{=}} \frac{1}{2}$

See N3 for factors.

To cancel you divide the top and bottom by the same number.

example

Change these fractions to eighths.

a $\frac{1}{2} = \frac{?}{8}$ b $\frac{3}{4} = \frac{?}{8}$ c $\frac{5}{8} = \frac{?}{8}$

a $\frac{1}{2} \overset{\times 4}{\underset{\times 4}{=}} \frac{4}{8}$ b $\frac{3}{4} \overset{\times 2}{\underset{\times 2}{=}} \frac{6}{8}$ c $\frac{5}{8} \overset{\times 1}{\underset{\times 1}{=}} \frac{5}{8}$

Multiply the top and bottom by the same number.

This rectangle is made from 12 squares.

$\frac{1}{4}$ is blue. $\frac{1}{4}$ of 12 is 3 squares.

$\frac{3}{4}$ is white. $\frac{3}{4}$ of 12 is 9 squares.

▶ To find $\frac{1}{4}$ you divide by 4.

▶ To find $\frac{3}{4}$ you divide by 4 then multiply by 3.

To find $\frac{1}{5}$ you divide by 5.

Exercise N5

1 Copy this diagram.

Shade $\frac{3}{4}$ of it.

2 There are 20 pieces in this block of chocolate.

  a Gillian wants to eat $\frac{1}{4}$ of the block.
    How many pieces is this?
  b Chris eats 10 pieces.
    What fraction is this of the complete block?

3 a Write down the fraction of each shape that is shaded.

    i   **ii**   **iii**   **iv**   **v**

  b Write down the fraction of each shape that is not shaded.

4 Find $\frac{1}{4}$ of £10.

5 a Cancel these fractions to their lowest form: $\frac{2}{10}, \frac{4}{10}, \frac{5}{10}, \frac{6}{10}, \frac{8}{10}$

  b Mark the positions of $\frac{1}{10}$ and $\frac{1}{5}$ on a copy of this number line.

6 Copy these diagrams. Fill in the missing values.

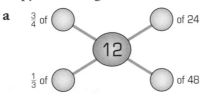   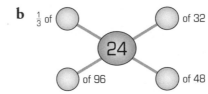

7 a Copy this diagram.
    Shade $\frac{1}{3}$ of it.
  b What fraction is unshaded?
    Simplify your answer if possible.

8 What is two-fifths of 100?

9 How many halves are there in 20?

10 Look at these fractions. Write them in their simplest form.

  a $\frac{30}{40}$ **b** $\frac{35}{40}$ **c** $\frac{36}{48}$ **d** $\frac{40}{45}$

11 Find the missing numbers.

  a $\frac{1}{2}$ of 100 = $\frac{1}{4}$ of ?   **b** $\frac{3}{4}$ of 20 = $\frac{1}{2}$ of ?

12 Look at this rectangle.

  a How many squares is $\frac{1}{2}$ of the rectangle?

  b How many squares is $\frac{1}{3}$ of the rectangle?

  c How many squares is $\frac{1}{6}$ of the rectangle?

  d Explain why $\frac{1}{2} + \frac{1}{3} + \frac{1}{6} = 1$.

You can write decimals as fractions using place value:

1	•	$\frac{1}{10}$	$\frac{1}{100}$
0	•	2	5

$$0.25 = \frac{2}{10} + \frac{5}{100} = \frac{20}{100} + \frac{5}{100} = \frac{25}{100} = \frac{1}{4}$$

(×10, ÷25 and reverse arrows shown)

▶ You should know these **equivalents**:

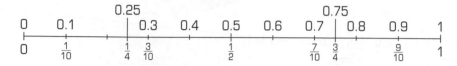

▶ You can write fractions as decimals by dividing:

$\frac{3}{20}$ means $3 \div 20 = 0.15$

You can use a calculator
or use equivalent fractions (N5):

$\frac{3}{20} = \frac{15}{100} = 0.15$ (×5)

▶ **Percentage** means 'out of 100'.

There are 100 squares.
36 squares are blue.
36% is blue.

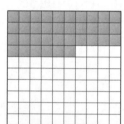

▶ You can write a percentage as a fraction:

36% means $\frac{36}{100} = \frac{9}{25}$ (÷4)

See N5 for how to cancel.

You write a fraction as a percentage by finding an equivalent fraction
with 100 on the bottom.

example

Your test result is $\frac{14}{25}$. David's test result is 24 out of 40.
Express each result as a percentage.

$\frac{14}{25} = \frac{56}{100} = 56\%$ (×4)

$\frac{24}{40} = \frac{6}{10} = \frac{60}{100} = 60\%$ (÷4, ×10)

You have 56%   David has 60%

Think: Percentage means something
out of 100 = $\frac{?}{100}$.

▶ You should know these equivalents:

0	0.1	0.2	0.3	0.4	0.5	0.6	0.7	0.8	0.9	1.0
0	10%	20%	30%	40%	50%	60%	70%	80%	90%	100%
0	$\frac{1}{10}$	$\frac{2}{10}$	$\frac{3}{10}$	$\frac{4}{10}$	$\frac{5}{10}$	$\frac{6}{10}$	$\frac{7}{10}$	$\frac{8}{10}$	$\frac{9}{10}$	1

▶ 50% means $\frac{1}{2}$. To find 50% you divide by 2.

▶ 25% means $\frac{1}{4}$. To find 25% you divide by 4.

▶ 10% means $\frac{1}{10}$. To find 10% you divide by 10.

To find 30% you find 3 × 10%.
30% of 50
  = 3 × 10% of 50
  = 3 × 5
  = 15

Exercise N6

L3 **1** Write any number that is bigger than one but smaller than two.

2 Copy this diagram.
  Shade 25% of it.

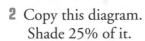

3 What percentages are the arrows pointing to?

L4 **4** What is 50% of £8?

5 A TV costs £80.
  What is the price after a reduction of 25%?

 6 Copy these diagrams. Fill in the missing values.

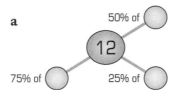 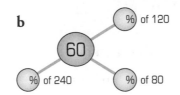

7 Mark is printing out his homework on a computer.
  He has printed 40% so far.
  Colour in a copy of this bar chart to show how much he has printed.

8 Convert these fractions to percentages.

  a $\frac{1}{10}$ **b** $\frac{1}{5}$ **c** $\frac{3}{10}$ **d** $\frac{3}{5}$ **e** $\frac{9}{10}$

L5 **9** 25% of a number is 50. What is the number?

 10 Maria's test score is 18 out of 30. What is her percentage?

11 Order these numbers from smallest to largest.

  $\frac{1}{4}$ 0.24   27% $\frac{13}{50}$

12 These are the results of a survey in Davina's class.
  There are 8 boys and 10 girls in the class.

  a What percentage of the girls travelled by car?
  b Copy and complete:
    25% of the boys travelled to school by _____.
  c Is walking to school equally popular for boys and girls?
    Explain your answer.

See D1 for two-way tables.

School journey	Boys	Girls
Walk	6	6
Car	2	3
Bus	0	1
	8	10

13 Choose the correct inequality (<, = or >) for these pairs
  of numbers.

< means less than
> means more than
= means equal to

  a 70% $\frac{3}{4}$ **b** $\frac{1}{3}$ 30%   **c** 35%   0.35

13

1 Write in figures the number six hundred and nine.

2 Gareth has some pegs and a pegboard.
He can make a rectangle with 18 pegs.

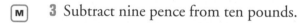

Gareth's rectangle is 6 pegs long and 3 pegs wide.

a Show how to use 18 pegs to make another
rectangle with a different shape.
The rectangle must be more than 1 peg long and more than 1 peg wide.
How many pegs long is your rectangle?
How many pegs wide is your rectangle?

Gareth cannot make a rectangle with 5 pegs.
He can only make a row.

This is because 5 is a prime number.

b Draw a row with a prime number of pegs which is greater than 5.
What is your prime number?
c Gareth says: 9 is a prime number.
Explain why Gareth is wrong.
You can write your answer, or draw a diagram

 3 Subtract nine pence from ten pounds.

4 Write a factor of sixty that is bigger than ten but smaller than twenty.

5 What is fifty per cent of twenty pounds?

6 Look at these three signs:

| < | = | > |
| is **less** than | is **equal** to | is **greater** than |

Examples:

| 5 < 6 | 4 − 3 = 2 − 1 | 6 − 2 > 9 − 6 |
| 5 is **less** than 6 | 4 − 3 is **equal** to 2 − 1 | 6 − 2 is **greater** than 9 − 6 |

Copy these number sentences and write the correct **sign**, < or = or > in each.
a 8 + 2 ...... 7 + 6
b 6 − 3 ...... 1 + 2
c 0   ...... −3
d −7   ...... −2

7 Here are some number cards:

Joan picked these three cards:
She made the number **314** with her cards.
a Which extra card should she pick to make
her number **10 times** as big?
What number is **10 times** as big as 314?

14

L4

b Andy has these cards:

He made the number 42.5 with four of his cards.
Use some of Andy's cards to show the number **10 times** as big as 42.5
Use some of Andy's cards to show the number **100 times** as big as 42.5

8 a Look at these fractions.

$\frac{1}{2}$　　$\frac{1}{3}$　　$\frac{5}{6}$

Mark each fraction on a copy of the number line.
The first one is done for you.

b Copy the fractions and fill in the missing numbers in the boxes.

$\frac{2}{12} = \frac{\Box}{6}$　　　　$\frac{1}{2} = \frac{12}{\Box}$　　　　$\frac{1}{\Box} = \frac{6}{24}$

L5 **M** **9** I am thinking of a two-digit number that is a multiple of eight.
The digits add up to six.
What number am I thinking of?

N3

M **10** Write a multiple of three that is bigger than one hundred.

N3

M **11** What number should you add to minus three to get the answer five?

N4

12 Look at these number cards:

a Choose a card to give the answer 4.

$\boxed{+2}$ + $\boxed{-5}$ + $\boxed{}$ = 4

b Choose a card to give the lowest possible answer.
Write the value on the card and the answer.

$\boxed{-2}$ + $\boxed{}$ =

N4

M **13** What is three-fifths of forty pounds?

N5

14 The table shows some percentages of amounts of money.

	£10	£30	£45
5%	50p	£1.50	£2.25
10%	£1	£3	£4.50

You can use the table to help you work out the missing numbers.

15% of £30　= £ ....
£6.75　　　　= 15% of £ ....
£3.50　　　　= .... % of £10
25p　　　　　= 5% of £ ....

▶ **Proportion** compares the size of a part to the size of the whole.

Out of 10 bricks there are
4 white, 1 grey and 5 blue bricks.

The proportion of white bricks is:
4 out of 10 or $\frac{4}{10} = \frac{2}{5}$ or $4 \div 10 = 0.4$ or 40%.
The proportion of grey bricks is:
1 out of 10 or $\frac{1}{10}$ or $1 \div 10 = 0.1$ or 10%.
The proportion of blue bricks is:
5 out of 10 or $\frac{5}{10} = \frac{1}{2}$ or $5 \div 10 = 0.5$ or 50%.

> You can express a proportion as a fraction, decimal or percentage.

▶ **Ratio** compares the size of two portions or parts with each other.

The ratio of white bricks to grey bricks is 4 : 1, so
For every 4 white bricks there is 1 grey brick.

> Ratios are always written using a colon, :

You can simplify ratios by dividing both numbers by a common factor.

example

Simplify these ratios.

a 6 : 12   **b** 6 : 9   **c** 36 : 16   **d** 15 : 20

a $\div 6 \left(\begin{array}{c} 6 : 12 \\ 1 : 2 \end{array} \right) \div 6$ **b** $\div 3 \left(\begin{array}{c} 6 : 9 \\ 2 : 3 \end{array} \right) \div 3$ **c** $\div 4 \left(\begin{array}{c} 36 : 16 \\ 9 : 4 \end{array} \right) \div 4$ **d** $\div 5 \left(\begin{array}{c} 15 : 20 \\ 3 : 4 \end{array} \right) \div 5$

> See N5 for how to cancel.

You can split quantities into different proportions using a ratio.

The ratio of orange to water in orange squash is 1 : 4.
This gives 1 + 4 = 5 parts of orange squash.

| O | W | W | W | W |

> $\frac{1}{5}$ of the drink is orange and $\frac{4}{5}$ is water

example

Share 30 sweets between Jason and Bhavna in the ratio 2 : 1.

The total number of parts is 2 + 1 = 3.
One part is 30 sweets ÷ 3 = 10 sweets.

| 10 | 10 | 10 |

So Jason gets 10 × 2 = 20 sweets and Bhavna gets 10 × 1 = 10 sweets.

> **Check:**
> 20 + 10 = 30 sweets

▶ When the ratio between two amounts is constant, the amounts are in **direct proportion**.

example

A 100 g jar of coffee costs £2.50.
What will 200 g cost?

£2.50

200 g = 100 g × 2
So the cost is £2.50 × 2 = £5.

L3 [M] **1** A class has 28 students. 14 are girls. What proportion is this?

2 In a bag of 20 sweets, 15 are toffees.
Give the proportion of toffees in the bag as:

   a a cancelled fraction
   b a decimal
   c a percentage.

3 One token is given away in every newspaper.
5 tokens are worth a free magazine.

   a How many free magazines can I get for 24 tokens?
   b How many tokens must I exchange for 3 magazines?

L4 [M] **4** Simplify the ratio 4 : 12.

5 In a game, each piece has a value

   2 horses = 6 soldiers   3 horses = 1 queen

   How many soldiers are equal to one queen?

[📇] **6** The clockwise angle from N to E is 90°.

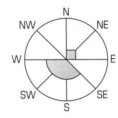

   a Calculate the clockwise angle from N to NE.
   b Calculate the clockwise angle from SE to W.

7 Simplify these ratios:

   a 15 : 3   **b** 2 : 20   **c** 5 : 30   **d** 7 : 21   **e** 88 : 11

[📇] **8** Which coffee jar is the best value? Explain your reasoning.

9 The ratio of land to water in the world is about 1 : 3.
What proportion is water? Give your answer as

   a a fraction
   b a percentage.

L5 [M] **10** If 3 chocolate bars cost 45p, what will 4 bars cost?

11 Reduce these ratios to their simplest form:

   a 10 : 15   **b** 21 : 28   **c** 16 : 24   **d** 9 : 15   **e** 20 : 32

12 These are the ingredients for scrambled eggs for 2 people.
List the ingredients for 3 people.

   100 ml of milk
   4 eggs

[📇] **13** Danny and Benny share £100 in the ratio 2 : 3.
How much does each boy receive?

► Addition and subtraction are **inverse** operations of each other.

$4 + 3 = 7$ means $7 - 3 = 4$ and $7 - 4 = 3$

► Multiplication and division are **inverse** operations of each other.

$4 \times 3 = 12$ means $12 \div 4 = 3$ and $12 \div 3 = 4$

► Multiplication is repeated addition.

$2 + 2 + 2 + 2 + 2 + 2 + 2 + 2 + 2 + 2 + 2 = 11 \times 2$

11 lots of 2

It is easier to multiply than to keep on adding.

► Division is repeated subtraction.

$12 \div 4$ means 'How many 4s are there in 12?'

$\left.\begin{array}{l} 12 - 4 = 8 \\ 8 - 4 = 4 \\ 4 - 4 = 0 \end{array}\right\}$ 3 lots of 4   3 lots of 4

Division and fractions are connected.
All these expressions mean the same:

example

Find:

a $\frac{1}{3}$ of £36   **b** $\frac{2}{3}$ of £36

----

a $36 \div 3 = 12$ **b** $\frac{1}{3}$ of $36 = 12$

so $\frac{2}{3}$ of $36 = 2 \times 12 = 24$

When there are several different operations you do them in this order:

1 **B**rackets
2 **I**ndices (powers)
3 **D**ivision and **M**ultiplication
4 **A**ddition and **S**ubtraction

See N4 for indices and powers.

The word BIDMAS will help you remember the **order of operations**.

Treat $\frac{4 \times 3}{3 + 3}$ the same as $(4 \times 3) \div (3 + 3)$.

example

Work out:

a $1 + 3 \times 2$ **b** $(2 + 3) \times 3$ **c** $4^2 + 2$ **d** $\frac{4 \times 3}{3 + 3}$

----

a $1 + 6$ **b** 5×3 **c** $16 + 2$ **d** $\frac{12}{6}$

$= 7$ $= 15$ $= 18$ $= 2$

($\times$ then $+$)   (brackets then $\times$)   (indices then $+$)   (brackets then $\div$)

BID**M**AS   **B**IDMAS   BID**M**AS   **B**IDMAS

1 Is 341 times 676 the same as 676 times 341?

2 Find the missing numbers.

    a $848 - ? = 321$
    b $? - 246 = 402$

3 Use this multiplication table to find the missing numbers.

    a $34 \times 22 = ?$

    b $19 \times 35 = ?$

    c $32 \times ? = 608$

    d $693 \div 33 = ?$

    e $735 \div ? = 35$

×	31	32	33	34	35
18	558	576	594	612	630
19	589	608	627	646	665
20	620	640	660	680	700
21	651	672	693	714	735
22	682	704	726	748	770

4 Decide if each statement is true or false.

    a $12 + 6 = 6 + 12$

    b $12 - 6 = 6 - 12$

    c $12 \times 6 = 6 \times 12$

    d $12 \div 6 = 6 \div 12$

5 The price of a DVD is halved. It is now £8.
What price was it?

6 Calculate:
    a $(3 + 2) \times 6$ **b** $3 + (2 \times 6)$

7 Find the value of these.
    a $\frac{1}{3}$ of £15   **b** $\frac{2}{3}$ of £15

> See N5 for fractions

8 Complete these statements using $+$, $-$, $\times$, $\div$.

    a $3 \quad 5 = 10 \quad 2$ **b** $12 \quad 3 = 10 \quad 6$

    c $4 \quad 4 = 5 \quad 4$ **d** $3 \quad 3 = 18 \quad 2$

> You need to use two operations

9 Copy these statements and put brackets to make them correct.

    a $3 + 4 + 2 \times 3 = 27$ **b** $3 + 4 + 2 \times 3 = 21$

10 Parminder and Martin count the number of square slabs on a patio.
Parminder adds:

$3 + 3 + 3 + 3 + 3 + 3 + 3 + 3 + 3 + 3 + 3 + 3 + 3 + 3 + 3$

Martin adds:

$15 + 15 + 15$

Is there a quicker method to find the total number of slabs?

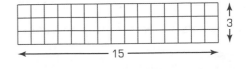

11 Work out $5^2 \times 2^2$.

> See N4 for indices.

12 Copy this multiplication grid.
Fill in the missing numbers.

×			6
3	6	12	18
	10		30
	14	28	42

13 Calculate:

    a $\frac{8 \times 14}{7 \times 2}$ **b** $\frac{9 \times 24}{8 \times 8}$

14 How can I check that $8.25 \div 15 = 0.55$?
Give a multiplication that will check this answer.

You can use **partitioning** and **compensation** to add and subtract mentally.

example

Work out:

a $34 + 58$

b $79 - 31$

a **Partitioning**
Split both numbers into tens and units:

$34 = 30 + 4$ $58 = 50 + 8$
Add the tens: $30 + 50 = 80$
Add the units: $4 + 8 = 12$
So $34 + 58 = 80 + 12 = 92$

b **Compensation**
Write the second number to the nearest ten, subtract and then adjust the answer.
$31 = 30 + 1$
$79 - 30 = 49 \rightarrow 49 - 1 = 48$

If you know your multiplication facts you know your divisions.

$6 \times 8 = 48$ means $48 \div 6 = 8$ and $48 \div 8 = 6$

Learn the multiplication facts up to 10×10 from the table.

You can use these facts to work out larger multiplications in your head.

×	1	2	3	4	5	6	7	8	9	10
1	1	2	3	4	5	6	7	8	9	10
2	2	4	6	8	10	12	14	16	18	20
3	3	6	9	12	15	18	21	24	27	30
4	4	8	12	16	20	24	28	32	36	40
5	5	10	15	20	25	30	35	40	45	50
6	6	12	18	24	30	36	42	48	54	60
7	7	14	21	28	35	42	49	56	63	70
8	8	16	24	32	40	48	56	64	72	80
9	9	18	27	36	45	54	63	72	81	90
10	10	20	30	40	50	60	70	80	90	100

example

Work out 36×7.

Partition 36 into tens and units: $36 = 30 + 6$
Multiply the tens: $30 \times 7 = 210$ (using $3 \times 7 = 21$)
Multiply the units: $6 \times 7 = 42$
So $36 \times 7 = 210 + 42 = 252$

Approximate first:
$30 \times 7 = 210$
so $36 \times 7 \approx 250$

You can use partitioning and compensation to mentally **double** and **halve**.

example

a Double 59.

b Halve 58.

a **Partitioning**
Split 59 into tens and units:
$59 = 50 + 9$
Double the tens: $50 \times 2 = 100$
Double the units: $9 \times 2 = 18$
So double $59 = 100 + 18 = 118$

b **Compensation**
Round to the nearest ten:
$58 = 60 - 2$
Half of $60 = 30$
Half of $2 = 1$
So half of $58 = 30 - 1 = 29$

To multiply by 4, double and double again.

To multiply by 8, double, double and double again.

To divide by 4, halve and halve again.

▶ To multiply by 5, multiply by 10 and then halve. $36 \times 5 = 360 \div 2 = 180$

▶ To divide by 5, divide by 10 and then double. $240 \div 5 = 24 \times 2 = 48$

Exercise N9

L3 [M] **1** Divide thirty-two by four.

[M] **2** Add thirty-six and forty-eight.

[M] **3** Double twenty-eight.

[M] **4** Multiply nine by four.

[M] **5** Stamps come in books of four.
I need twenty-four stamps.
How many books do I need?

[M] **6** Work out $1 + 2 + 3 + 4 + 5 + 6 + 7 + 8 + 9$.

L4 [M] **7** Multiply twenty-five by ten.

[M] **8** Find fifty per cent of fifty pounds.

[M] **9** Divide fifty-four by nine.

[M] **10** Add together these numbers.

| 31 | 43 | 27 |

[M] **11** Multiply seven by six.

[M] **12** What is three-quarters of twenty?

[M] **13** The pie chart shows the proportion of students who are under 14.
What percentage of students is over 14?

[M] **14** 10% of £9 is 90p. What is 5% of £9?

[M] **15** Subtract thirty-seven from eighty-one.

[M] **16** Add seventy-six and eighty-eight.

[M] **17** Calculate the value of thirteen times seven.

[M] **18** Find the value of x if $2x + 1 = 11$.

See A1 for substitution.

[M] **19** Work out $4 \times 2 \times 5$.

L5 [M] **20** Calculate the area of this square.

12 cm

[M] **21** What is two-fifths of thirty-five?

[M] **22** Calculate the value of thirty-four times six.

[M] **23** Work out 16×25.

[M] **24** Divide two hundred by eight.

[M] **25** How many quarter hours are there in two and a half hours?

[M] **26** Look at this calculation: $24 \times 36 = 864$
Use it to work out the answer to 2.4×3.6.

See N1 for place value.

To add or subtract whole numbers and decimals, each digit must be in its correct place value position.

KEYWORDS
Addition   Difference
Subtraction

example

Work out:

a 328 + 2547   b 321 − 89
c 8.4 − 0.05   d £5 − 47p

a

1000	100	10	1
	3	2	8
+ 2	5	4	7
2	8	7	5
		1	

Add/subtract the columns starting from the right.

b

100	10	1
²3̸	¹¹2̸	¹1̸
−	8	9
2	3	2

c

1	.	$\frac{1}{10}$	$\frac{1}{100}$
8	.	³4̸	¹0
− 0	.	0	5
8	.	3	5

Line up the decimal points. Fill any gaps with zeros.

d

1	.	$\frac{1}{10}$	$\frac{1}{100}$
⁴5̸	.	⁹¹0̸	¹0
− 0	.	4	7
4	.	5	3

Remember
47p = £0.47

Use approximations to check your answers:
a 300 + 2500 = 2800
b 300 − 100 = 200
c 8.4 − 0.1 = 8.3
d £5 − 50p = £4.50

▶ To find the **difference** between two numbers you subtract:

The difference between 100 and 40 is 100 − 40 = 60.

example

The attendances for class A and class B are shown in the table.
Calculate the difference of the total weekly attendance between the two classes.

	Mon	Tues	Wed	Thu	Fri
Class A	24	21	25	26	27
Class B	27	20	27	28	29

Total for class A = 24 + 21 + 25 + 26 + 27 = 123
Total for class B = 27 + 20 + 27 + 28 + 29 = 131

The difference is 131 − 123 = 8.

Take the smaller number from the larger number.

example

Find the length of the spade.

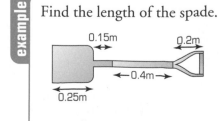

0.15m   0.2m
←0.4m→
0.25m

1	.	$\frac{1}{10}$	$\frac{1}{100}$
0	.	2	5
0	.	1	5
0	.	4	
+ 0	.	2	
1	.	0	0
₁		₁	

The length is exactly 1 metre.

Exercise N10

L3

1 Calculate the perimeter of this triangle.

85 mm   126 mm
187 mm

See S9 for perimeter

2 Work out: **a** 64 + 19   **b** 87 − 19

3 a Find the total cost of the shopping.
  b How much change is there from a £20 note?

4 Add together 237 and 325.

5 Subtract 253 from 619.

6 Find the difference between 36 and 18.

7 The results of a survey are shown.

	Early	On time	Late
Bright Buses	36	24	8
Charlie's Coaches	4	12	13

How many more Bright Buses than Charlie's Coaches are there?

L4

8 Calculate: **a** 432 + 3269   **b** 801 − 168

9 Find the sum of 8355 and 866.

10 Find the difference between 327 and 510.

11 Work out 18 + 1.8 + 0.18.

12 In these diagrams the numbers in the circles add up to the number in the rectangle. Find the missing numbers.

a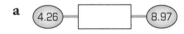

b

13 Calculate the unknown lengths.

a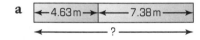

b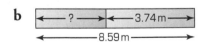

14 Shahid's height is 1.74 m. His son's height is 1.8 m. How much taller is his son?

L5

15 What do you add to 4.5 to make 7.4?

16 What do you subtract from 8.9 to make 3.6?

17 Find the number that is halfway between 3.5 and 5.7.

18 In this diagram, the numbers in the end circles add up to give the numbers in the rectangles. Find the values of **a**, **b** and **c**.

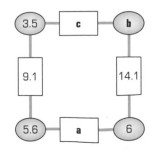

Multiplication and division

▶ To **multiply** whole numbers you can either use the **standard method** or the **grid method**.

KEYWORDS
Estimate   Multiplication
Decimal place   Division

example

Work out:

a 328×7 **b** 328×17

a Standard method

```
      3   2   8
  ×           7
  _____
      5   6        7 × 8
  1   4   0        7 × 20
2   1   0   0      7 × 300
  _____
2   2   9   6
```

b Grid method

×	300	20	8
10	3000	200	80
7	2100	140	56

```
      3000
       200
        80
      2100
       140
  +     56
      ____
      5576
         1
```

Check by approximating:
a $300 \times 7 = 2100$
b $300 \times 20 = 6000$

You can also use the standard method or the grid method to multiply **decimals**.

example

Work out 3.28×7.

Work out 328×7 using the standard method or grid method as above.
Then position the decimal point to make the answer about 21 $(3 \times 7 = 21)$.
$328 \times 7 = 2296$
So $3.28 \times 7 = 22.96$

You can use your approximation to help place the decimal point.

▶ You can use repeated subtraction to divide.

example

Work out: **a** $405 \div 9$ **b** $40.5 \div 9$

a
```
    _____
  9)405
  − 360      9 × 40
    ____
     45
  −  45      9 × 5
    ____
      0
```

$9 \times 45 = 405$ so $405 \div 9 = 45$

b Work out $405 \div 9$ as in part **a**, and then position the decimal point so that the answer is about 4 $(40 \div 10 = 4)$.
$405 \div 9 = 45$
$40.5 \div 9 = 4.5$

Check by approximating:
a $400 \div 10 = 40$
b $40 \div 10 = 4$

example

Share £26.10 between 18 people.

First work out $2610 \div 18$.
```
    _____
  18)2610
  − 1800      18 × 100
    _____
     810
  −  720      18 × 40
    _____
      90
  −   90      18 × 5
    _____
       0
```

So $18 \times 145 = 2610$
This means
$2610 \div 18 = 145$.

As $26.10 \div 18$ is approximately 1.5, you know:
£26.10 ÷ 18 = £1.45.

Check by approximating:
$30 \div 20 = 1.5$

If you have a remainder, think carefully about the number of decimal places you need to give. For money, always give two: £1.45.

Exercise N11

L3

1 Work out: **a** 46 × 5 **b** 136 ÷ 4

2 Find the cost of 5 audio cassettes at £1.25 each.

3 Multiply 54 by 4.

4 Divide 255 by 5.

5 18 sweets are to be shared equally by 4 people.
   a How many sweets will each person have?
   b How many sweets will be left over?

6 Multiply 156 by 3.

L4

7 Divide 861 by 7.

8 Work out: **a** 24 × 24 **b** 32 × 23

9 Find the total cost of 25 stamps.
   Each stamp costs 28p.

10 Work out 7 × 8 × 9.

11 Three tins of beans and a loaf of bread cost £1.80.
   The loaf costs 84p.
   How much is one tin of beans?

12 Calculate: **a** 9.7 × 6 **b** 8.7 × 7

13 Work out: **a** 6.3 ÷ 7 **b** 6.3 ÷ 6

14 Find the cost of 15 bars of chocolate at 95p each.

15 A TV can be bought for 15 payments of £14 or £200 cash.
   Which is the cheaper option and by how much?

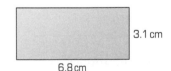

L5

16 Emily works for 18 hours.
   She is paid £4.20 each hour.
   How much does she earn?

17 Calculate the area of this rectangle.

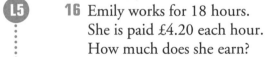

3.1 cm

6.8 cm

18 a A 24-week bus pass costs £336.
      How much is this per week?
   b A 52-week bus pass costs £650. How much is this per week?
   c Which pass is the better value? Explain your reasoning.

19 Calculate 26.4 ÷ 15.

20 Here is a section of fencing.
   Each upright post is 0.75 m long.
   Each horizontal length is 1.8 m long.
   a If there are 8 uprights and 2 horizontals, find the
      total length of wood needed to build this fence.
   b The price of the wood is £2.40 per metre.
      What is the total cost of the wood?

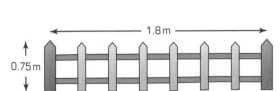

1.8 m

0.75 m

It is easy to make mistakes using a calculator.
Always check by approximating the answer.

KEYWORDS

Calculator   Approximate
Display   Check

example

Find the cost of three shirts
at £8.65 each.

Input 8.65 ⨯ 3 =
Display 25.95
So the cost is £25.95.

The order you press the keys depends
on the type of calculator you have.
Use the examples to check you
know how your calculator works.

Check:
9 × 3 = 27

▶ Use the √ key to work out **square roots**.
To find √1024:
Input 1024 √ =
Display 32.

Check:
30 × 30 = 900

Work out **percentage** problems by converting to a decimal.

example

Find 8% of £14.25.

Input 0.08 ⨯ 14.25 =
Display 1.14
So 8% of £14.25 is £1.14.

8% = 8 ÷ 100 = 0.08

Check:
10% of 15 = $\frac{1}{10}$ of 15 = 1.5

▶ Use the +/– key to enter negative numbers.

example

The temperature was ⁻1 °C.
It then dropped by 5 °C.
What is the new temperature?

Input 1 +/– – 5 =
Display ⁻6
The new temperature is ⁻6 °C.

To input ⁻1 into some calculators
you have to press +/– and then 1.
Some calculators display -6
as 6-.

Be careful with calculations involving money.
You also need to take care with divisions:

6.5 means £6.50
6.05 means £6.05

example

There are 71 students doing PE.
How many groups of four are there?
How many students are left?

Input 71 ÷ 4 =
Display 17.75
There are 17 full groups.

To find how many students are left, find the number of students
in 17 groups:
17 × 4 = 68, and then subtract from
the total number of students: 71 − 68 = 3.

Check:
70 ÷ 2 = 35
35 ÷ 2 = 17.5

Exercise N12

L3

1 Paula's shopping bill is £4.70. She gives a £20 note.
How much change should she receive?

2 Find the cost of 14 CDs at £4.70 each.

3 a Multiply 3.4 by 2.5, than add 4.6.
  b How much less than 5.4 is 1.5 × 1.5?

4 a Add up these weekly shopping bills:
    £53.35, £46.80, £93.47 and £75.08.
  b Is this total less than or more than £250?
    By how much?

5 Find the cost of:

  a 2 cups of tea and a cake
  b a tea, a coffee and a biscuit
  c one of each item.

Tea	£1.25
Coffee	£1.30
Cake	75p
Biscuit	90p

L4

6 1000 people are to travel by coach to the seaside.
Each coach can carry 45 people.

  a How many coaches are needed?
  b How many spare seats are there?

7 Find the missing numbers in these diagrams.
For example:

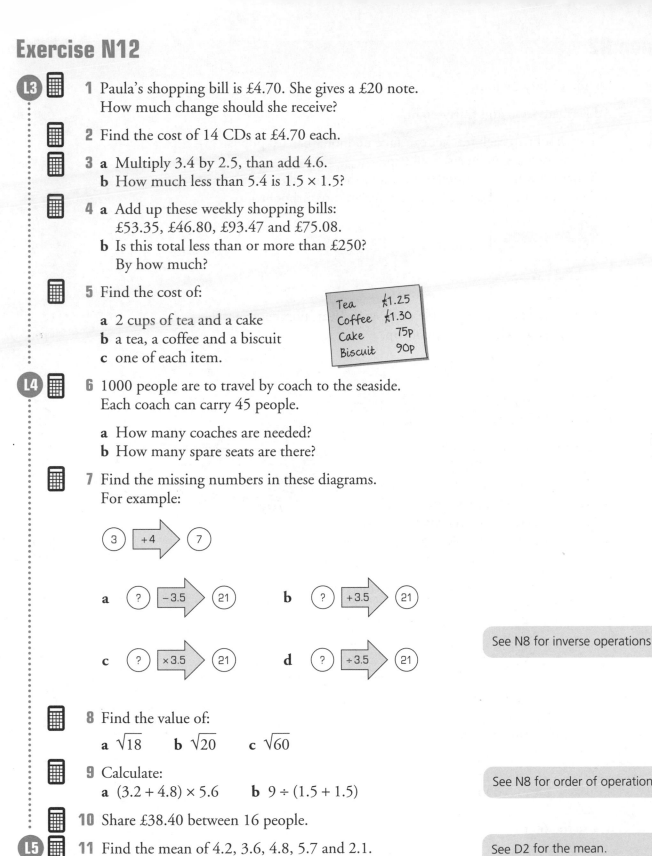

$3 \rightarrow +4 \rightarrow 7$

a $? \rightarrow -3.5 \rightarrow 21$ **b** $? \rightarrow +3.5 \rightarrow 21$

c $? \rightarrow \times 3.5 \rightarrow 21$ **d** $? \rightarrow \div 3.5 \rightarrow 21$

> See N8 for inverse operations

8 Find the value of:
  a $\sqrt{18}$ **b** $\sqrt{20}$ **c** $\sqrt{60}$

9 Calculate:
  a $(3.2 + 4.8) \times 5.6$ **b** $9 \div (1.5 + 1.5)$

> See N8 for order of operations.

10 Share £38.40 between 16 people.

L5

11 Find the mean of 4.2, 3.6, 4.8, 5.7 and 2.1.

> See D2 for the mean.

12 Calculate:
  a 6% of £42   **b** $17\frac{1}{2}$% of £36.40

13 A bottle holds 2 litres of lemonade.
A glass holds 225 ml.
How many full glasses can I expect to pour?
How much will be left in the bottle?

> See S10 for liquid measures.

14 A maths book has 96 pages.
$12\frac{1}{2}$% of the pages are on algebra.
How many pages is this?

1 Divide twenty by four.

2 Add seventy-two and thirty-eight.

 3 On a school trip each teacher can take no more than 20 pupils.

    a Three teachers go on a school trip.
       What is the greatest number of pupils they can take with them?

    b The table shows how many pupils go on three school trips.

Number of pupils	Number of teachers
100	
104	
199	

    Copy and complete the table to show the least number of teachers
    that must go with each school trip.

4 **a** Add together 156 and 417.
    b Subtract 192 from 638.
    c Multiply 56 by 3.
    d Divide 130 by 5.

 5 There are 15 rulers in a box.
    A box of rulers costs £1.45.

    a How many rulers are there in 8 boxes?
    b How much do 8 boxes cost?
    c How much do 30 rulers cost?
    d How many boxes of rulers could you buy for £7.25?

15 Rulers   £1.45

 6 Copy the calculations.
    Use +, −, × or ÷ to make each calculation correct.

    5 .... 2 = 10 3
    12 .... 3 = 3 3
    2 .... 1 = 9 3
    6 .... 6 = 7 7

Examples
$$2 + 4 = 7 - 1$$
$$5 \times 3 = 3 \times 5$$

7 Here is the 65 times table.

    a Copy these calculations.
       Use the 65 times table to help you fill in the missing numbers.

       65   ×   5 = ...
       390   ÷   65 = ...
       12   ×   65 = ...
       20   ×   65 = ...

    b Use the 65 times table to help you work out 16×65
       Show how you do it.

$1 \times 65 = 65$
$2 \times 65 = 130$
$3 \times 65 = 195$
$4 \times 65 = 260$
$5 \times 65 = 325$
$6 \times 65 = 390$
$7 \times 65 = 455$
$8 \times 65 = 520$
$9 \times 65 = 585$
$10 \times 65 = 650$

8 **a** Copy these calculations and write the answers.
       $(4 + 2) \times 3 =$
       $4 + (2 \times 3) =$

    b Work out the answer to
       $(2 + 4) \times (6 + 3 + 1)$

    c Copy the calculation.
       Put brackets in to make the answer 50.
       $4 + 5 + 1 \times 5$

    d Copy the calculation again.
       Now put brackets in to make the answer 34.
       $4 + 5 + 1 \times 5$

L4 **9** Subtract nought point seven five from six.

10 Work out
238 + 1487 = ...
723 − 154 = ...

11 There are two small tins and one big tin on these scales.
The two small tins each have the same mass.
The mass of the big tin is 2.6 kg.
What is the mass of one small tin?
Show your working.

12 a A club wants to take 3000 people on a journey to London.
The club secretary says: We can go in coaches. Each coach can carry **52** people.
How many coaches do they need for the journey?
Show your working.
b Each coach costs £420.
What is the total cost of the coaches?
c How much is each person's share of the cost?

L5 **13** Screenwash is used to clean car windows.
To use Screenwash you mix it with water.

Winter mixture	**Summer mixture**
Mix **1** part Screenwash with **4** parts water.	Mix **1** part Screenwash with **9** parts water.

a In winter, how much water should I mix with 150 ml of Screenwash?
b In summer, how much Screenwash should I mix with 450 ml of water?
c Is this statement correct?

> **25%** of **winter** mixture is **Screenwash**.

Explain your answer.

14 Twenty-five per cent of a number is seven.
What is the number?

15 How many nought point fives are there in ten?

16 a A shop sells plants.
Find the cost of 35 plants.
Show your working.

95p each

b The shop sells trees.
Mr Bailey has £250.
He wants to buy as many trees as possible.
How many trees can Mr Bailey buy?
Show your working.

£17 each

In algebra, letters are used to represent numbers.
You can add the same letters together.

▶ $n + n + n + n$ is 4 lots of n or $4 \times n$ or $n \times 4$.
You write this as $4n$.

You can also multiply letters.

▶ $x \times y$ is written xy.
$x \times x$ is written x^2.

▶ To find the value of an **expression** you substitute the value of the letter.

example

Find the value of these expressions when $d = 10$.

a $3d$ **b** $2d + 4$ **c** d^2

---

a $3d = 3 \times 10$ **b** $2d + 4 = 2 \times 10 + 4$ **c** $d^2 = 10^2$
$= 30$ $= 24$ $= 100$

When $d = 10$, $3d$ means 3×10.

In an expression, **like terms** have the same letters.
You can **simplify** expressions by adding or subtracting like terms.

example

Simplify these expressions.

a $a + 2a + 5a$ **b** $a + b + 3a + 2b$ **c** $a + 5 + 2a + 7$

---

a $a + 2a + 5a$ **b** $a + b + 3a + 2b$ **c** $a + 5 + 2a + 7$
$= 8a$ $= a + 3a + b + 2b$ $= a + 2a + 5 + 7$
                        $= 4a + 3b$ $= 3a + 12$

a means $1 \times a$

To multiply out brackets you multiply each term inside the bracket by
the number in front of the bracket:

$8 \times 53 = 8 \times (50 + 3) = 8 \times 50 + 8 \times 3$
$\qquad = 400 + 24$
$\qquad = 424$

	50	3
8	8×50	8×3

See N11 for multiplying brackets.

It's exactly the same in algebra.

example

Simplify these expressions.

a $5(n + 6)$ **b** $(a + b) \times c$

---

a $\quad 5(n + 6) = 5 \times n + 5 \times 6$
$\qquad\qquad = 5n + 30$

	n	6
5	$5 \times n$	5×6

b $(a + b) \times c = a \times c + b \times c$
$\qquad\qquad = ac + bc$

	a	b
c	ac	bc

Equal expressions have the same value.

example

$4(x + 3) = 4x + 12$
Check this equality for $x = 7$

$4(7 + 3) = 4 \times 10 = 40$
$4 \times 7 + 12 = 28 + 12 = 40$

Exercise A1

 L4 [M] **1** Find the value of $3x$ if $x = 4$.

[M] **2** Find the value of $d + 6$ if $d = 4$.

3 If $d = 4$, find the value of these expressions.

   a $d + 3$ **b** $4d$ **c** $2d + 5$ **d** $\frac{d}{2}$ **e** d^2

4 Work out the value of the expression $5n - 3$ when:

   a $n = 1$ **b** $n = 10$ **c** $n = 0$

5 Simplify these expressions.

   a $n + n + n + n$
   b $3n + n$
   c $3n - 2n + 5n$

6 Calculate the perimeter of these shapes when $p = 3$ cm and $q = 4$ cm.

  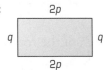

> See S11 for perimeter.

7 Multiply out the brackets in these expressions.
   a $2(x + 4)$ **b** $3(x + 2)$ **c** $8(x + 10)$

8 Your age is $2ab$, where $a = 1$ and $b = 7$. Is this true?
Explain your reasoning.

9 The numbers in the circles add up to the number in the rectangle.
Write expressions for the missing numbers.

   a    **b**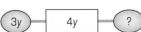

 L5 **10** Check this equality for $x = 4$.
$5(x + 2) = 5x + 10$.

11 Simplify $a + 2b + 3a$.

12 The teacher says 'If n is 4, what is $6n$?'
Siobhan says '64'.
Kieren says '24'.
Niamh says '10'.
Who is correct and why?

13 Find a value of d so that all the cards are equal.

14 Simplify these expressions.
   a $2t + 3 + 3t$
   b $8d + 4 + d - 1$
   c $k + 1 - k - 1$

15 In this number tower, you add two adjacent
bricks to get the number in the brick above.
What is the value of the top brick?

If you represent a number by a letter, you can describe other numbers using the same letter.

If n represents a number:

▶ $2n$ is 2 times bigger than the number,
▶ $n + 4$ is 4 more than the number,
▶ $n - 3$ is 3 less than the number,
▶ n^2 is the number multiplied by itself.

> **example**
>
> If you are a years old now, how old will you be in 3 years time?
>
> ....
>
> You will be $a + 3$ years old.

Check:
If you are 14 now, you'll be 17 in 3 years time:
$a + 3 = 14 + 3 = 17$

You can process information by using a **formula**.

> **example**
>
> A rectangle has width w and length l.
> **a** Construct a formula for the perimeter, P, of the rectangle.
> **b** Find P if $l = 10$ and $w = 5$.
>
> ....
>
> **a** $P = l + w + l + w$
> $= 2l + 2w$
> **b** $P = 2 \times 10 + 2 \times 5 = 30$

A diagram will help:

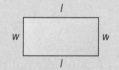

See S11 for perimeter.

A formula can be expressed in words or letters.

> **example**
>
> To change inches to centimetres you multiply by 2.54.
> **a** Change 36 inches to centimetres.
> **b** Is 36 inches more or less than one metre?.
>
> ....
>
> **a** 36 inches $= 36 \times 2.54$ cm
> $= 91.44$ cm
> **b** 91.44 cm < 100 cm so 36 inches is less than one metre.

See S9 for measures of length.

▶ An **equation** links two or more expressions using an equals ($=$) sign.

$x + 2 = 8$ is an equation.

Solving an equation means finding the value of the unknown.

> **example**
>
> The sum of angles in a triangle is 180°.
> **a** Form an equation for the angles in this triangle.
> **b** Solve the equation to find the angles marked a.
>
>
>
> ....
>
> **a** $a + a + 38° = 180°$
> $2a + 38° = 180°$
> **b** Use inverse operations:
> $2a + 38° = 180°$
> $2a = 180° - 38° = 142°$ (the opposite of $+$ is $-$)
> $a = 142° \div 2 = 71°$ (the opposite of $\times$ is $\div$)
>   The unknown angles are 71°.

See S1 for angle sum of a triangle.

Check:
$2 \times 71° + 38° = 180°$

Exercise A2

L3 **1** I think of a number. I add seven. The answer is ten.
What was my number?

2 Look at the equation: $a + b = 10$.
When $b = 7$, what is the value of a?

3 Solve these equations:
a $a + 5 = 15$ **b** $2b = 12$ **c** $c - 1 = 3$

4 Write down the formula for the area of this rectangle.

5 The time taken to microwave scrambled eggs is given by the rule
'1 minute for each egg, then add 2 minutes'.
a How long should you cook 3 eggs?
b How long should you cook n eggs?

6 Solve these equations:
a $2x + 1 = 17$ **b** $3y - 1 = 8$

 7 This formula changes miles to kilometres:
miles = kilometres × 0.625
Change 8 kilometres to miles.

8 Write down an expression for the number that is:
a 3 times bigger than n
b 3 times the number n add 5.

9 I think of a number. I call it n. I subtract 2 from my number.
Write an expression to show the result.

 10 Look at this equation: $\frac{b}{3} = 10$
What is the value of b?

11 This formula changes a Celsius (C) temperature to a Fahrenheit (F) temperature:
$F = C × 9 ÷ 5 + 32$
Change these temperatures to Fahrenheit:
a 100 °C   **b** 0 °C   **c** 20 °C

12 Ross earns £P every hour. He works for h hours.
The amount of money he earns is W.
Write down a formula for W in terms of P and h.

13 Solve these equations: **a** $8x - 11 = 85$ **b** $5x + 9 = 74$

14 The numbers in the circles add up to the numbers in the rectangles.
State whether the following statements are true or false.

a $p + q = k$
b $g - r = p$
c $q - r = h$

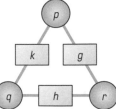

15 Form and solve an equation to find the value of a in this triangle.

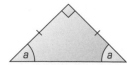

See S1 for angle sum of a triangle

▶ A **sequence** is a set of numbers that follow a **rule**.
Each number in a sequence is called a **term**.

Here are the first six terms of some well-known sequences.

See N3 and N4 for definitions of these terms.

> **KEYWORDS**
> Number sequence   Term
> Position   Rule

Even numbers: 2, 4, 6, 8, 10, 12, ...
Odd numbers: 1, 3, 5, 7, 9, 11, ...
Square numbers: 1, 4, 9, 16, 25, 36, ...
Multiples of 5: 5, 10, 15, 20, 25, 30, ...

You can show some number sequences in diagrams:

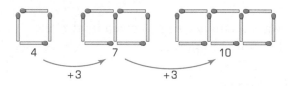

Number of matches   4   7   10
                        +3   +3

The rule is 'add 3'.

▶ You use a **term-to-term rule** to find the next term from the previous term.

example

a Find the next two terms in this sequence.

2,   5,   8,   11,   14,   __,   __
  +3   +3   +3   +3   +3   +3

b The rule for a sequence is 'start with 19 then subtract 2 each time'. Find the first five terms of the sequence.
....

a $14 + 3 = 17$, $17 + 3 = 20$

b 19,   17,   15,   13,   11
          −2   −2   −2   −2

▶ You use a **position-to-term rule** to find a term from its **position** in the sequence.

example

Blue and white tiles are arranged in patterns.

Pattern number: 1   2   3

Number of white tiles: 2   4   6

How many white tiles are in the 10th pattern?
....

The rule for the number of white tiles is:
'multiply the pattern number by 2'.
Number of white tiles in 10th pattern $= 2 \times 10 = 20$

The pattern number is the position.

▶ The **position-to-term rule** can be written as an equation.

example

The rule for a pattern is $T = 2n + 1$, where $n =$ pattern number.
Find the 8th term in the pattern.
....

$n = 8$ so $T = 2 \times 8 + 1$
                        $= 17$

Exercise A3

 1 What is the next number in this sequence? 10, 20, 30, 40, _____

2 Find the missing numbers on these number lines.

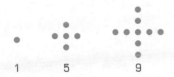

 3 What is the next number in this sequence? 1, 4, 9, 16, _____

4 Here is a sequence of patterns:

    a Draw the next two patterns in the sequence.
    b Count the number of dots in each pattern.
    c How many dots will there be in the 10th pattern?
       Give a reason for your answer.

5 a Write down the next two numbers in this sequence.
       1, 3, 6, 10, 15, _____, _____
   b What is the name of these numbers?
   c Draw diagrams for each term.

> See N4 for special numbers.

6 Here is a sequence of patterns.

    a Draw the next two patterns in the sequence.
    b Count the number of matchsticks in each pattern.
    c How many matchsticks will there be in the 10th pattern?
       Give a reason for your answer.

7 The rule for a sequence is 'start with 8, then add 5 to each term'.

    a Find the first five terms.
    b What is the 10th term?

8 The rule for a sequence is 'start with 1, then multiply each term by 10'.

    a Find the first five terms.
    b Is one million in this sequence? If so, which term is it?

 9 What are the missing numbers in this sequence? 7, _____, _____, 25, 31

10 The rule for a sequence is 'Multiply the position number by 2 and subtract 1'.

    a Copy and complete the table.

Pattern number	1	2	3	4	5
Term					

    b What is the 10th term in the sequence?

11 The rule for this pattern is $L = 7S + 1$
    where S is the number of squares,
         L is the number of lines.

    a How many lines are in the diagram with 5 squares?
    b Draw the diagram with 5 squares to check your answer.

▶ A **function machine** changes an **input** number to an **output** number according to a rule.

This function machine multiplies by 3 then adds 2:

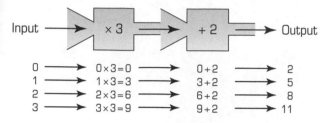

```
0 ———→  0×3=0  ———→  0+2  ———→   2
1 ———→  1×3=3  ———→  3+2  ———→   5
2 ———→  2×3=6  ———→  6+2  ———→   8
3 ———→  3×3=9  ———→  9+2  ———→  11
```

Given the output, you can work backwards using inverses to find the input.

The output of this function machine is 8. What was the input?

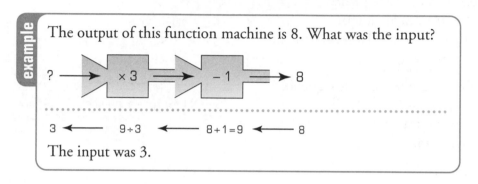

$3 \longleftarrow 9 \div 3 \longleftarrow 8 + 1 = 9 \longleftarrow 8$

The input was 3.

See N8 for inverses operations.

▶ You can use a **mapping diagram** to show several inputs and outputs.

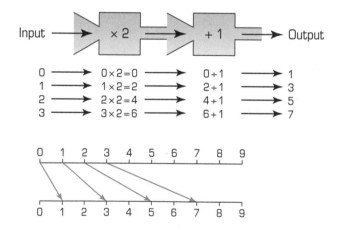

```
0 ———→  0×2=0  ———→  0+1  ———→  1
1 ———→  1×2=2  ———→  2+1  ———→  3
2 ———→  2×2=4  ———→  4+1  ———→  5
3 ———→  3×2=6  ———→  6+1  ———→  7
```

The **equation** of this function is $x \times 2 + 1 = y$ or $y = 2x + 1$.

▶ You can give input and output pairs as **coordinates** and plot them as a **graph**.

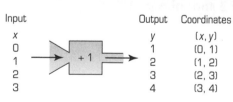

Input	Output	Coordinates
x	*y*	(*x*, *y*)
0	1	(0, 1)
1	2	(1, 2)
2	3	(2, 3)
3	4	(3, 4)

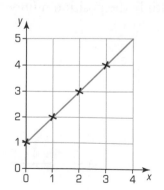

See S6 for coordinates.

The **equation** of this function is $x + 1 = y$ or $y = x + 1$.

Exercise A4

L3 M

1 The number 5 is input into this function machine. What is the output?

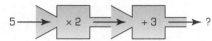

2 Input these numbers into the function machine. Write the output in each case.

   a 1   **b** 2   **c** 3   **d** 4   **e** 5

L4 M

3 The number 5 is input into this function machine. What is the output?

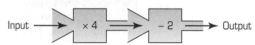

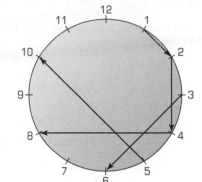

4 The arrows connect pairs of numbers, using the same rule each time.

   a What number will the arrow from 6 connect to?
   b What is the rule?

5 Input these numbers into the function machine. Write down the output in each case.

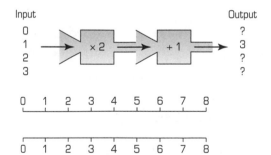

   a 0   **b** 1   **c** 2   **d** 3   **e** 4

6 There are many rules that change 4 to 12. Complete these sentences to show some of the rules.

   a add ____
   b multiply by ____
   c multiply by 2 then ____
   d multiply by 5 then ____

7 Write the rule for the function machine that makes $7 \rightarrow 3$ and $11 \rightarrow 7$.

8 a Find the missing outputs for the function.

Input		Output
0		?
1		3
2		?
3		?

0 1 2 3 4 5 6 7 8

   b Draw a mapping diagram of the function.

0 1 2 3 4 5 6 7 8

L5 M

9 Write this function using an equation.

10 a Complete the values of y for the function $y = x + 3$.

x		y	Coordinates
0			(0,)
1	$\rightarrow$	4	(1, 4)
2			(2,)
3			(3,)

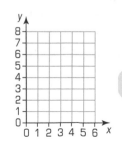

See S6 for coordinates

   b Plot the graph of the function on a grid like this one.

► You use **conversion graph** to convert units of measure.
The graph will always be a straight line.

example

Construct a conversion graph for miles and kilometres.
5 miles ≈ 8 km
0 miles = 0 km
Use your graph to convert these distances.

  a   10 miles to kilometres   **b**   65 km to miles

See S9 for measures of length.

Reading from the
graph:

  a   10 miles is
about 16 km.
  b   65 km is about
41 miles.

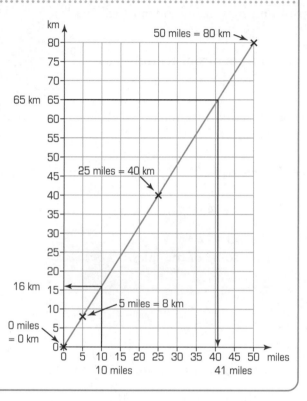

Check:
The points lie on a straight line.

Check:
50 miles is 80 km so
10 miles is 16 km (÷5).

► A **graph of charges** can be used to work out costs.
The graph will always be a straight line.

example

This formula gives the cost of hiring a DVD.

   Cost = £2 + £1 for every day

Construct a graph of charges.

  a   Use your graph to find the cost of hiring a DVD for 5 days.
  b   How many days hire would be possible for £8?

Generate some points to plot:
1 day   Cost = £2 + £1 × 1 = £3
2 days   Cost = £2 + £1 × 2 = £4
3 days   Cost = £2 + £1 × 3 = £5

Reading from the graph:

  a   £7
  b   6 days

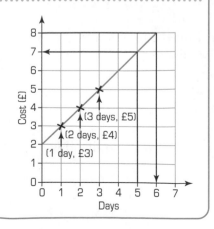

Check:
The points lie on a straight line.

Exercise A5

L3

1 The graph shows the cost of bed and breakfast for one person.

   a What is the cost for 1 day?
   b What is the cost for 3 days?

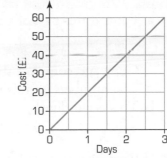

L4

2 This graph shows °C and °F temperatures.
Use the conversion graph to estimate:

   a 10 °C in °F
   b 35 °C in °F
   c 70 °F in °C
   d 40 °F in °C
   e normal body temperature of 37 °C in °F.

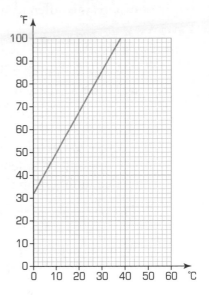

3 This graph shows the cost of buying packets of biscuits.
Use the graph to find:

   a the cost of 1 packet
   b the cost of 6 packets
   c the number of packets you can buy with 80p
   d the number of packets you can buy with £1.40
   e the cost of 10 packets.

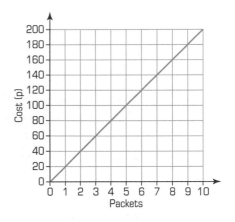

L5

4 The graph shows the cost of a taxi at Tony's Taxis.

   a What is the cost of a 6-mile journey?
   b How far can I travel with £4?

Carol's Cars charge as follows:

> £5 call out plus £1 a mile

   c Copy and complete the table.

Number of miles	1	2	3	4	5	6	7	8	9	10
Total cost (£)	6									

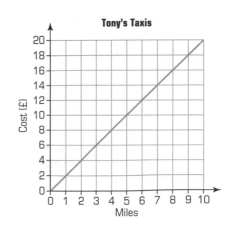

Tony's Taxis

   d Copy the graph for Tony's Taxis and then draw the graph for Carol's Cars on it.
   e For how many miles is the cost the same for Tony's Taxis and Carol's Cars?

L3

1 a Look at this part of a number line:

Copy and complete this sentence:
The numbers on this number line go up in steps of ....

b This is a different number line.

Copy the number line and fill in the 3 missing numbers.

c This is a different number line.

Copy the number line and fill in the 3 missing numbers.

d This is a different number line.

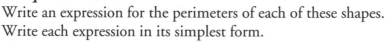

Copy the number line and fill in the 2 missing numbers.
Copy and complete this sentence:
The numbers on this number line go up in steps of ....

A3

L4

2 The perimeter of this shape is $3t + 2s$.

$$p = 3t + 2s$$

Write an expression for the perimeters of each of these shapes.
Write each expression in its simplest form.

a **b** **c** **d**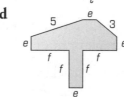

A3

3 a I can think of three different rules to change 6 to 18.
Copy and complete these sentences to show what these rules could be.
first rule: add ....
second rule: multiply by ....
third rule: multiply by 2 then ....

b Now I think of a new rule.
The new rule changes 10 to 5 and it changes 8 to 4.
Write what the new rule could be.

A2

M **4** $a + b = 20$. When a is seven, what is the value of b?

A2

5 A book shows two ways to change °C to °F

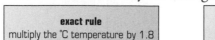 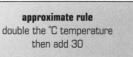

Copy and complete:
a Using the exact rule, 25 °C is ....°F
Using the approximate rule, 25 °C is ....°F
b Using the exact rule, 0 °C is ....°F
Using the approximate rule, 0 °C is ....°F
c Show that at 10 °C, the exact rule and the approximate rule give the same answers.

A2

L4

6 Some pupils throw two fair six-sided dice. Each dice is numbered 1 to 6.
One dice is blue. The other dice is red.
Anna's dice show blue 5, red 3.
Her total score is 8.
The cross on the grid shows her throw.

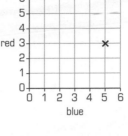

a Carl's total score is 6.
What numbers could Carl's dice show?
Copy Anna's grid.
Put crosses on the grid to show all the
different pairs of numbers Carl's dice could show.

b The pupils play a game.
Winning rule: Win a point if the number on the blue dice is the same as the number on the red dice.
Copy Anna's grid again.
Put crosses on the grid to show all the different winning throws.

c The pupils play a different game.
The grid shows all the different winning throws.

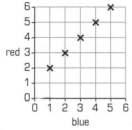

Copy and complete the winning rule:
Winning rule: Win a point if the number on the blue dice is

....

A4

L5 **7 a** You pay £2.40 each time you go swimming.
Copy and complete the table.

Number of swims	0	10	20	30
Total cost (£)	0	24		

b Copy these axes.
Now show this information on the graph.
Join the points with a straight line.

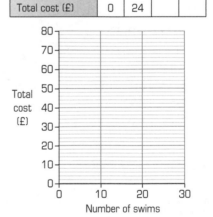

c A different way of paying is to pay a yearly fee
of £22.
Then you pay £1.40 each time you go swimming.
Copy and complete the table.

d Now show this information on the same graph.
Join these points with a straight line.

Number of swims	0	10	20	30
Total cost (£)	22	36		

e For how many swims does the graph show that the cost is the same for
both ways of paying?

A5

8 Write each expression in its simplest form.
a $7 + 2t + 3t$
b $b + 7 + 2b + 10$

A1

M **9** Look at the equation $\frac{k}{2} = 20$. Solve it to find the value of k.

A2

M **10** I am thinking of a number. I call it n. I add five to my number.
Write an expression to show the result.

A2

The **line segments** AB and CD are parallel.

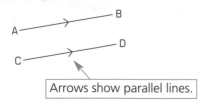

PQ and RS are perpendicular. They intersect at right angles.

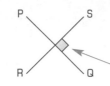

The square shows the right angle.

▶ An angle is a measure of turn.

A quarter turn is 90°

A half turn is 180°

A full turn is 360°

This **angle** is written ∠DEF, angle DEF, DÊF or angle E. It is less than 90°. It is about 45°.

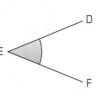

▶ A **polygon** is a closed shape with 3 or more straight edges.

A **triangle** is a polygon with 3 sides and 3 angles.

These marks show equal sides.

A triangle with 2 equal sides and 2 equal angles is **isosceles**.

A triangle with 3 equal sides and 3 equal angles is **equilateral**.

A triangle with no equal sides or angles is **scalene**.

A **right-angled triangle** has a right angle.

▶ The angles in a triangle add up to 180°.

example

Calculate the missing angles in this isosceles triangle.

....

$a + a + 70° = 180°$ (angles in a triangle sum to 180°)
    $2a + 70° = 180°$
          $2a = 110°$ so $a = 55°$

Check:
$55 + 55 + 70 = 360°$

▶ Angles at a point add to 360°.

$a + b + c + d = 360°$

Angles on a straight line add to 180°.

$a + b + c = 180°$

Vertically opposite angles are equal.

example

Find angles a, b and c.

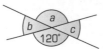

....

$a = 120°$ (vertically opposite angles are equal)
$b = 60°$ (angles on a straight line add to 180°)
$c = 60°$ (either of the two reasons above)

Check:
$60° + 120° + 60° + 120° = 360°$

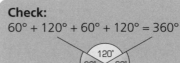

Exercise S1

1 What is the mathematical name of a regular triangle?

M **2** What is the angle between two perpendicular lines?

3 Copy these triangles. Indicate equal sides if there are any.

   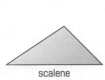

a   b   c   d

isosceles   right-angled   equilateral   scalene

4 Write the angle shown on each compass.

a   b   c

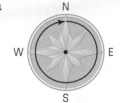 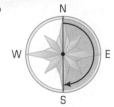 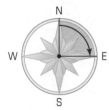

L4 M   **5** What is the sum of the angles in a triangle?

6 Calculate the size of each unknown angle. Give a reason in each case.

a   b   c

  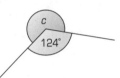

d   e   f

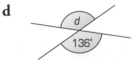  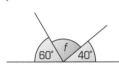

7 Copy the diagram.
Draw a line that is:
a perpendicular to PQ
b parallel to PQ.

P ———————— Q

8 Use the diagram to write:
a the length of side AB
b the size of angle B
c the size of angle BÂC
d the type of triangle ABC.

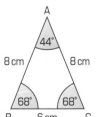

L5 M   **9** The angles in an isosceles triangle are x, x and 80°. Find the value of x.

10 Calculate the size of the unknown angles. Give a reason in each case.

a   b   c

 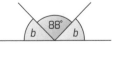

d   e   f

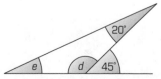 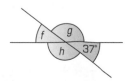

Quadrilaterals and 2-D representations

▶ **Quadrilaterals** have 4 sides and 4 angles.

Square
All sides and angles equal.
Opposite sides parallel.

Kite
Adjacent sides equal.
No parallel sides.
One pair of opposite angles equal.

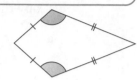

Rectangle
Opposite sides equal
and parallel.
All angles equal.

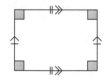

Isosceles trapezium
One pair of opposite sides equal
and parallel.

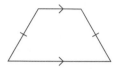

Parallelogram
Opposite sides equal
and parallel.
Opposite angles equal.

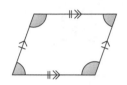

Trapezium
No sides or angles equal.
One set of opposite sides parallel.

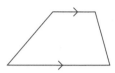

Rhombus
All sides equal.
Opposite sides parallel.
Opposite angles equal.

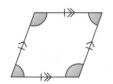

Arrowhead (delta)
Two pairs of adjacent sides equal.
No parallel sides.

▶ The angles in a quadrilateral add up to 360°.

example

Calculate the missing angles in this kite.

$$a + a + 90° + 30° = 360°$$
$$2a + 120° = 360°$$
$$2a = 240°$$
$$a = 120°$$

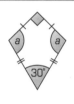

Check:
120° + 120° + 30° + 90° = 360°

▶ A **net** is a 2-D shape that can be folded to form a 3-D shape.

You should know these 3-D shapes and their nets:

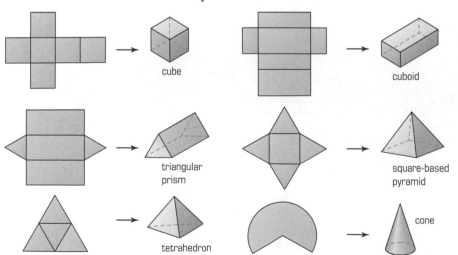

cube

cuboid

triangular prism

square-based pyramid

tetrahedron

cone

The faces of a cube are **congruent**. That means they are all the same shape and size.

You can draw many 3-D shapes on isometric paper.
Draw uprights upright!

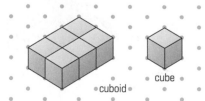

cuboid

cube

Exercise S2

1 What size is the angle at the corner of a square?

2 Copy the diagrams and indicate any parallel lines.

a trapezium   b rectangle   c parallelogram   d kite

3 A cuboid is cut as shown. Give the name of the new interior face in each case.

a   b   c

4 What is the sum of the angles in a quadrilateral?

5 a Draw the diagonal AD in this regular hexagon.
b Give the mathematical name of the two congruent shapes that are formed.

6 Rearrange the two congruent triangles to make:

a a square
b a parallelogram.

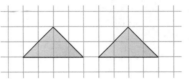

> Congruent triangles are the same shape and size.

7 Three cubes are joined together as shown.
Draw a different arrangement of the three cubes on isometric paper.

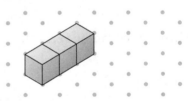

8 Calculate the size of the unknown angle in this quadrilateral.

9 Name the quadrilateral that has 4 equal sides, but no right angles.

10 Copy and complete this diagram so that the shaded part is the net of a cube.

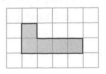

11 Which net folds to make this triangular prism?

    a   **b**   **c**

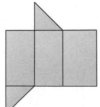 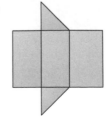 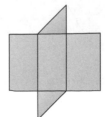

▶ A **reflection** gives the mirror image of an object.

Corresponding points on the object and image are **equidistant** from the mirror line.

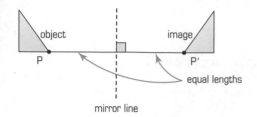

KEYWORDS
Reflection   Object
Image   Mirror line
Line symmetry
Reflection symmetry

Equidistant means the same distance.

You can find the position of the image:

▶ using a mirror
▶ using tracing paper
▶ by folding along the mirror line.

In a reflection the image is congruent with the object.

example

a Reflect the shape in the mirror line.
Indicate equal angles and equal lengths in the new shape.

b Name the quadrilateral formed by the object and its image.

....

a

b It is an isosceles trapezium.

Mirror lines can be vertical, horizontal or sloping.

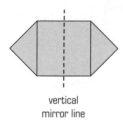

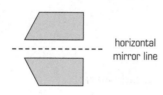

horizontal mirror line

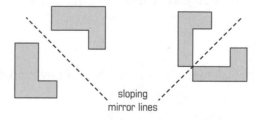

sloping mirror lines

vertical mirror line

It is easier to work with a vertical mirror line.
If necessary, rotate the page until the mirror line is vertical.

▶ A shape has **reflection symmetry** (or **line symmetry**) if one half of the shape is an exact mirror image of the other half.

Some shapes have one line of symmetry.

Some shapes have more than one line of symmetry.

Some shapes have no line of symmetry.

Exercise S3

 M   **1** What shape do you get if you fold this page down the middle?

2 Copy these shapes and draw the lines of symmetry.

   a   **b**    **c** 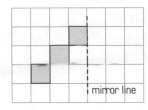   **d**

3 Copy the diagram and shade three more squares so that the dotted line is a mirror line.

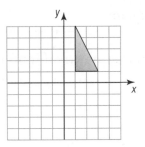

mirror line

 M   **4** State the number of lines of symmetry for an equilateral triangle.

See S1 for the meaning of equilateral.

5 Copy these shapes and draw the lines of symmetry if there are any.

   a   **b**   **c**   **d**

6 Copy the diagram and draw the triangle after:

   a a reflection in the *y*-axis
   b a reflection in the *x*-axis.

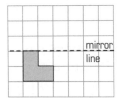

7 Copy the diagram and draw the 'L' shape after a reflection in the dotted mirror line.

mirror line

8 Copy the diagram and shade three triangles so that there are three lines of symmetry.

9 State the number of lines of symmetry for a regular octagon.

See S1 for the meaning of regular

10 Copy these shapes and draw all the lines of symmetry.

   a   **b**

11 The kite ABCD is folded along the dotted line. Copy and complete:

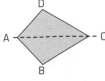

   a Triangles ABC and ADC are congruent because _____
   b Side AB = side _____   **c** Side BC = side _____
   d Angle B = Angle ___

See S2 for the meaning of congruent

12 Copy the 'L' shape and draw its reflection in the dotted line.

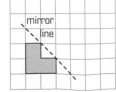

▶ A **rotation** turns an object through an angle about a point called the centre of rotation.

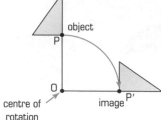

This rotation is 90° clockwise about O.

Length OP = Length OP'

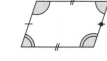

You can use tracing paper to find the position of the image.

> **example**
>
> **a** Rotate the shape through 180° about the dot.
> Indicate equal angles and equal lengths on the new shape.
> **b** Name the quadrilateral formed by the object and its image.
>
>
>
> **a**
>
> **b** It is a parallelogram.

Clockwise means turn the same direction as clock hands.
The other way is anticlockwise.

In a rotation the image is congruent to the object.

▶ A shape has rotational symmetry if it fits onto itself more than once in a 360° turn.

order 2   order 2   order 3

▶ The **order of rotational symmetry** is the number of times the shape fits onto itself during a 360° turn.

order 5   order 3   order 1

Count the start **or** the end position but not both.

> **example**
>
> **a** What is the order of rotational symmetry of each of these quadrilaterals?
>
>
>
> **b** How many lines of symmetry do they have?
>
> **a** Square 4, parallelogram 2, isosceles trapezium 1, rectangle 2
> **b**
>
>
>
> Square 4   Parallelogram 0   Isosceles trapezium 1   rectangle 2

See S3 for reflection symmetry.

Exercise S4

1 When the letter S is rotated half a turn, the letter fits exactly on top. Find the other letters with this property.

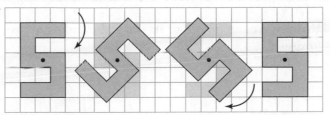

2 Draw this rectangle after a clockwise quarter turn.

3 Give the order of rotational symmetry for these signs.

a    b   c   d   e   f

4 This grid is rotated about the dot. Show the grid after:

  a a quarter turn clockwise
  b a further quarter turn clockwise.

5 Make two copies of this grid.

  a Shade two squares so that the grid has rotational symmetry of order 2.
  b Shade four squares so that the grid has rotational symmetry of order 2.

6 Draw a shape with rotational symmetry of order 1.

7 Name a shape that has 4 lines of symmetry and rotational symmetry of order 4.

8 Copy this triangle.
Rotate it through a quarter turn anticlockwise about the dot.

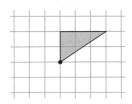

9 State the order of rotational symmetry of a regular hexagon.

10 Triangle A is rotated to triangle B.

  a Give the coordinates of the centre of rotation.
  b Give the angle of rotation.

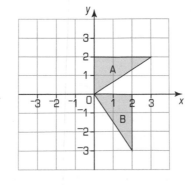

See S6 for coordinates

11 Copy this diagram. Shade in two more squares so that the grid has 4 lines of symmetry and rotational symmetry of order 4.

12 What is the order of rotational symmetry of a regular decagon?

▶ A **translation** moves an object to its image by sliding across then up or down.

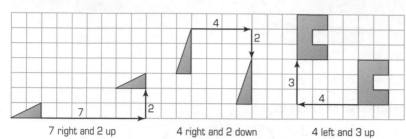

7 right and 2 up   4 right and 2 down   4 left and 3 up

The shapes slides across the grid.

example

Draw the image of this shape after a translation of 3 left and 2 down.

Choose a point on the shape to fix the position of the translated shape:

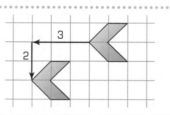

In a translation the image is congruent with the object.

▶ A transformation that changes the size of a shape is an **enlargement**.

The new shape is **similar** to the original shape.

Similar means the same shape but a different size.

The number the original lengths are multiplied by is the **scale factor** of the enlargement.

example

Enlarge these shapes using a scale factor of **2**.

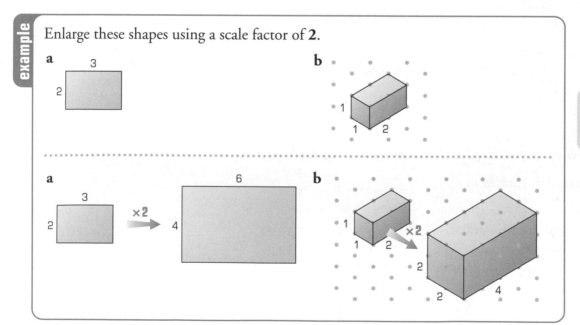

All the lengths have been multiplied by **2**.

▶ Shapes tessellate when they fit together without leaving any gaps.

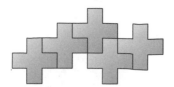

They must not overlap.

Exercise S5

1 Do squares tessellate?

2 Start at a point on the squared grid.
Follow these instructions to draw a pattern.
The first one is done for you.

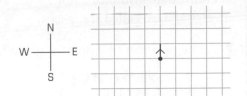

   a Move 1 square North
   b Then 1 square East
   c Then 2 squares South
   d Then 2 squares West
   e Then 3 squares North
   f Then 3 squares East

3 A person walks 3 m North, then 3 m West, then 3 m South, then 3 m East.
What is the shape of the path?

4 Copy the grid and draw the triangle after a translation of
4 right and 2 up.

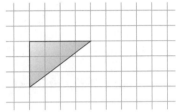

5 Draw a diagram to show how the four L shapes fit into the square.

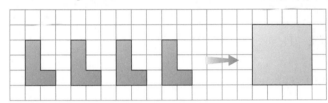

6 Copy the grid and draw the triangle after a translation of
3 left and 2 down.

7 On a grid, draw the square after these translations.

   a 2 right and 0 up
   b 4 right and 0 up
   c 6 right and 0 up
   d 0 right and 2 down
   e 2 right and 2 down

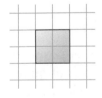

8 Replace the two translations of 8 right then 4 left with a
single translation.

9 Describe fully the transformation of:

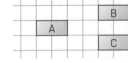

   a A to B
   b B to C
   c C to A

10 Four congruent parallelograms join to make a bigger
parallelogram. Copy the diagram and draw three more
parallelograms to complete the large parallelogram.
What is the scale factor of the enlargement?

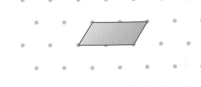

A coordinate grid has: a horizontal axis, called the *x*-axis, and a vertical axis, called the *y*-axis.

KEYWORDS

Coordinates   Horizontal

Axes   Origin

Vertical   Quadrant

▶ The position of a point is given by its **coordinates**.

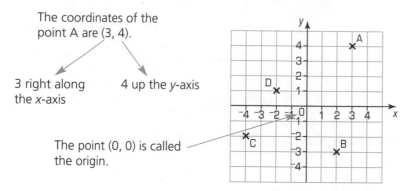

The coordinates of the point A are (3, 4).

3 right along the *x*-axis   4 up the *y*-axis

The point (0, 0) is called the origin.

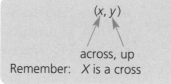

(x, y)

across, up

Remember: *X* is a cross

▶ Negative numbers in coordinates mean you go back or down.

The coordinates of the point C are ($^-$4, $^-$2).

4 back along the *x*-axis   2 down the *y*-axis

B is (2, $^-$3)
D is ($^-$2, 1)

example

a Plot and join these points: ($^-$3, $^-$1), (3, $^-$1), (1, 3), ($^-$1, 3).
b Name the shape.
c Give the coordinates of the midpoint of each side.

a

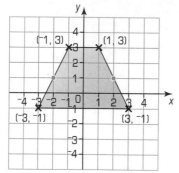

Each point is in a different **quadrant** or quarter of the grid.

b One pair of opposite sides is parallel.
The other pair of opposite sides are equal.
It is an isosceles trapezium.

See S2 for quadrilaterals.

c The midpoints are (0, $^-$1), ($^-$2, 1), (0, 3) and (2, 1).

example

L-shaped tiles are placed in a row on a grid.
a Write down the coordinates of the dots for the first five tiles.
b Write down the coordinates of the dot for tile 10.
Explain your reasoning.

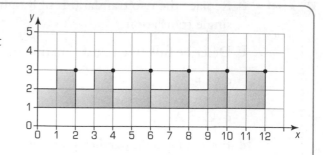

a (2, 3)   (4, 3)   (6, 3)   (8, 3)   (10, 3).
b (20, 3).
The *x*-coordinate is double the tile number. The *y*-coordinate is always 3.

Exercise S6

L3 **M** **1** Write down the coordinates of the point A.

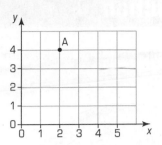

2 Write down the coordinates of:

a the point B
b the midpoint of AC
c the midpoint of BC
d the midpoint of AB.

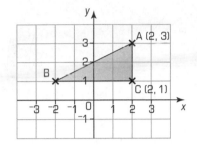

L4 **3** The coordinates of the points are:
(2, 1), (4, 2), (6, 3).

a Write down the coordinates of the next two points in the pattern.
b Write down the coordinates of the 10th point in this pattern.
Explain how you got your answer.
c Has this pattern got a point at (25, 12)? Explain your answer.

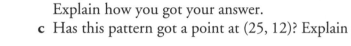

M **4** Write down the coordinates of the midpoint of BC.

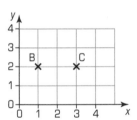

5 The parallelogram is reflected in the mirror line.
Give the coordinates of the reflection of the point A.

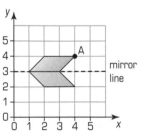

L5 **M** **6** The point (3, 3) is marked on the grid.
Write the coordinates of any other point on the straight line.

See S2 for quadrilaterals

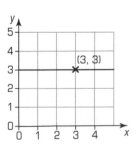

M **7** Write down the coordinates of any point on the *x*-axis.

8 Three points are marked on the grid. Name the shape that is formed, if the fourth point is:

a ($^-$2, 0)   **b** (4, 0)   **c** ($^-$3, $^-$1)
d ($^-$4, 0)   **e** (0, 2)

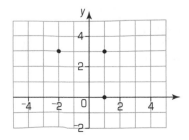

53

▶ You measure and draw angles with a protractor.

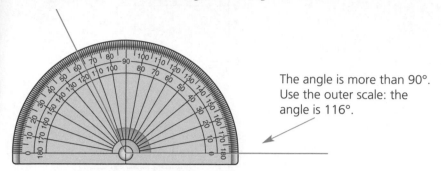

The angle is more than 90°. Use the outer scale: the angle is 116°.

There are two scales. Measure from 0 and use the correct scale. Estimate first.

To measure an angle bigger than 180°:

measure the smaller angle   then subtract from 360°.

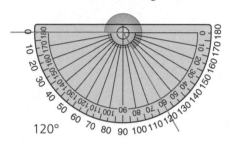

120°

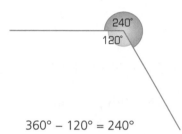

240°
120°

360° − 120° = 240°

You should know these definitions:
Acute angle: less than 90°
Right angle: 90°
Obtuse angle: more than 90°, less than 180°
reflex angle: more than 180°

You use compasses to draw arcs and circles:

You can construct a triangle accurately when you know:

Two sides and the included angle   Draw one side.   Use a protractor to draw the angle.   Measure the length you need.   Join the points.

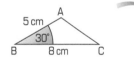

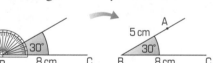

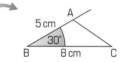

Two angles and the included side   Draw the side.   Use a protractor to draw one angle.   Draw the other angle.   Mark where the lines meet.

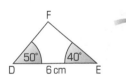

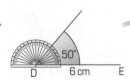

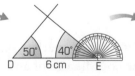

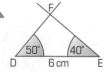

Three sides   Draw the longest side   Use compasses to draw an arc from one end.   Draw an arc from the other end.   Join the arcs to the line.

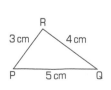

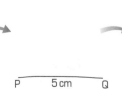

3 cm arc

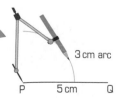

4 cm arc

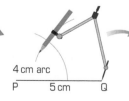

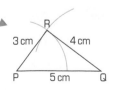

Exercise S7

  1 How many degrees are there in a right angle?

2 Measure the lengths of these lines in:

a cm   b mm

3 Measure these angles to the nearest degree.

a

b

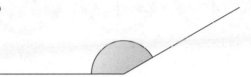

4 Measure this angle to the nearest degree.

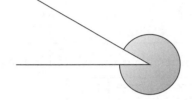

5 Draw a semicircle with a diameter of 8 cm.

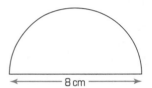

6 Draw this diagram accurately.

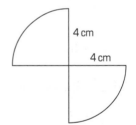

7 Construct this triangle using a ruler and protractor.

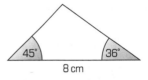

8 Construct this net of a pyramid using a ruler, protractor and compasses.

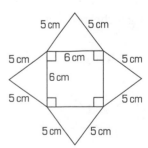

9 Construct this net of a cone using ruler, protractor and compasses.

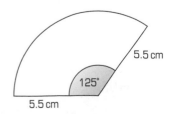

Time, temperature and scales

▶ There are 24 hours in a day.
An analogue clock is numbered from 1 to 12.

You use am for times before midday and pm for times after midday.

12 h clock	8.00 am	10.30 am	2.30 pm	8.00 pm
24 h clock	0800	1030	1430	2000

KEYWORDS

Time   Division
Scale   Temperature

24-hour clock times are the same as 12-hour clock times in the morning.

After midday, you add 12 to the 12-hour clock time to get the 24-hour clock time.

Learning these facts will help you solve problems:

60 seconds = 1 minute   24 hours = 1 day   52 weeks = 1 year
60 minutes = 1 hour   7 days = 1 week   12 months = 1 year

> **example**
>
> Part of a bus timetable is shown. Fill in the missing time.
>
> | Centre square | 09.35 | 09.55 | 10.15 |
> |---|---|---|---|
> | School lane | 09.47 | 10.07 | ? |
>
> Each journey lasts 12 minutes.
> The missing time is 10.15 + 12 minutes = 10.27.

On measuring instruments you need to check what each division is worth before you read the scale.

The scale shows 400 g.   5 divisions = 500 g
1 division = 100 g (÷5)
                                4 divisions = 400 g (×4)

Check:
400 g is between 0 g and 500 g.

The scale shows 3.8 cm.   10 divisions = 1 cm
1 division = 0.1 cm (÷10)
                                 8 divisions = 0.8 cm (×8)

Check:
3.8 cm is between 3 cm and 4 cm.

Temperature is measured using a thermometer.

This thermometer shows normal body temperature of 37.0 °C.

You measure in degrees Celsius (°C) or degrees Fahrenheit (°F)

The temperature on a warm day is about 20 °C.

> **example**
>
> Use the flow chart to change 37.0 °C to °F.
>
> °C → ×1.8 → +32 → °F
>
> 37.0 × 1.8 + 32 = 66.6 + 32 = 98.6
> 37.0 °C = 98.6 °F

See A4 for function machines

Exercise S8

L3 **M** **1** I arrive at the bus stop at 7.45 am.
The bus doesn't leave until 0810.
How many minutes do I have to wait?

2 **a** What measure is the arrow pointing to on this scale?

b Copy the scale and mark 40 cm on it.

3 What measure is the arrow pointing to?

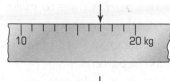

L4 **4** What measure is the arrow pointing to?

5 The thermometer shows the temperature at midday.

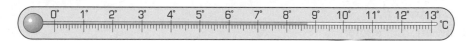

See N10 to add and subtract decimals.

The temperature was 3.9 °C at 8 o'clock.
What is the temperature rise?

6 Times are not the same in every city. The table gives the time differences from London for some cities.
If it is 3.00 pm in London, what time is it in:

a Paris
b New York
c Moscow?

City	Time
Paris	1 hour ahead of London
New York	5 hours behind London
Moscow	3 hours ahead of London

M **7** Jodi starts a journey at half past seven. It lasts one and a half hours.
What time does she finish?

8 Write the values shown on each measuring instrument:

a    **b** 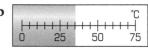   **c**

L5 **9** This scale measures °C and °F.

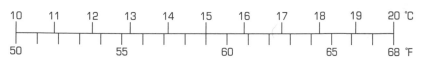

a 15 °C is about how many °F?
b 51 °F is about how many °C?
c To convert °C to °F, you multiply by 1.8 and add 32.
Check your answer to **a** using this method.

See A2 to use a formula in words

L3

1 Copy these groups of lines onto square dotty paper.
Reflect each group of lines to make a pattern.
You may use a real mirror or tracing paper to help you.

a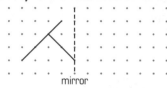
mirror

mirror

b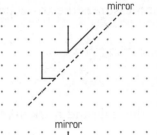

c Now use two mirror lines to make a pattern.
Copy the diagram onto square dotty paper.
First reflect the group of lines in one mirror
line to make a pattern.
Then reflect the whole pattern in the other
mirror line.

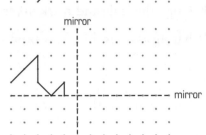
mirror

mirror

S3

M

2 Two different lines are parallel.
How many times do these lines touch?

S1

3 Look at these six angles.
a Which is the smallest angle?
b One of the angles is a right angle.
Which is a right angle?
c One of the angles is an obtuse angle.
Which is an obtuse angle?

A

B

C

D

E

F

S7

L4

4 a The time on this clock is 3 o'clock.
What is the size of the angle between the hands?
b Copy this sentence.
Use a whole number to complete it.
At .... o'clock the size of the angle between the hands is 180°
c What is the size of the angle between the hands at 1 o'clock?
d What is the size of the angle between the hands at 5 o'clock?
e How long does it take for the minute hand to move 360°?

S1

5 Look at the shaded shape.
a Two statements below are correct.
Write the letters of the correct statements.
A The shape is a quadrilateral.
B The shape is a trapezium.
C The shape is a pentagon.
D The shape is a kite.
E The shape is a parallelogram.
b What are the coordinates of point B?
c The shape is reflected in a mirror line.
Point A stays in the same place.
Where is point B reflected to? Give the coordinates.
d Now the shape is **rotated**.
Point A stays in the same place. Where is point B
rotated to? Give the coordinates.

S2

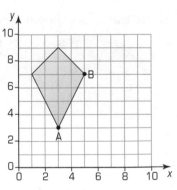

S6

S4

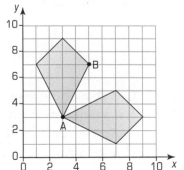

S4

L4 [M] **6** A robot moves one metre north, then one metre east, then one
metre south, then one metre west.
What is the name of the shape of the robot's path?

(S2)
(S5)

L5 **7** On this square grid, A and B must not move.
When C is at (6, 6), triangle ABC is isosceles.
  a C moves so that triangle ABC is still isosceles.
  Where could C have moved to?
  Write the coordinates of its new position.
  b Then C moves so that triangle ABC is isosceles
  and right-angled.
  Where could C have moved to?
  Write the coordinates of its new position.

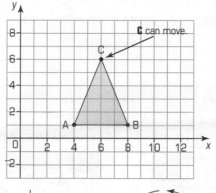

(S1)
(S10)

8 An equilateral triangle has 3 lines of symmetry.

It has rotational symmetry of order 3

Write the letter of each shape in the correct space
in a copy of the table.
You may use a mirror or tracing paper to help you.
The first two shapes have been written in for you.

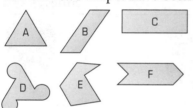

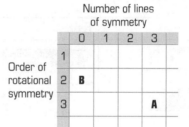

		Number of lines of symmetry			
		0	1	2	3
Order of rotational symmetry	1				
	2	**B**			
	3				**A**

(S3)
(S4)

9 a I have a paper circle.
  Then I cut a sector from the circle. It makes this net.
  Which 3-D shape below could I make with my net?

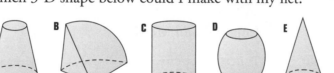

  b Here is a sketch of my net.
  Make an **accurate drawing** of my net.

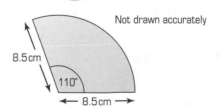

Not drawn accurately

8.5 cm
110°
8.5 cm

(S2)

10 Use compasses to construct a triangle that has sides 8 cm, 6 cm and 7 cm.
Leave in your construction lines.
Start with a horizontal line 8 cm long.

11 This cuboid is made from 4 small cubes.
  a On dotty isometric paper, draw a cuboid which is twice as high,
  twice as long and twice as wide.
  b Graham made this cuboid from 3 small cubes.
  Mohinder wants to make a cuboid which is twice as high, twice as
  long and twice as wide as Graham's cuboid.
  How many small cubes will Mohinder need altogether?

(S1)
(S3)

Lengths are measured using a ruler or tape measure.

This line measures 8.7 cm or 87 mm.

Lengths can be given in metric units.

millimetres (mm)	centimetres (cm)	metres (m)	kilometres (km)
1 mm is about the size of a grain of sugar.	1 cm is about the width of your fingernail.	2 m is about the height of a door.	1 km takes about 15 minutes to walk.

Lengths can also be given in imperial units.

inches	feet	yards	miles
1 inch ≈ $2\frac{1}{2}$ cm	1 foot is 12 inches 1 foot ≈ 30 cm	1 yard is slightly larger than the width of a door.	Balloons can fly at a height of 1 mile.

You need to know how metric and imperial units are related:

▶ **Metric**

10 mm = 1 cm
100 cm = 1 m
1000 m = 1 km

Imperial

12 inches = 1 foot
3 feet = 1 yard
1760 yards = 1 mile

Imperial and Metric

1 inch ≈ $2\frac{1}{2}$ cm
1 yard is a little less than 1 m.
5 miles ≈ 8 km

≈ means approximately equal to

example

Use the flow chart to change:

a 4 inches to centimetres
b 100 cm to inches

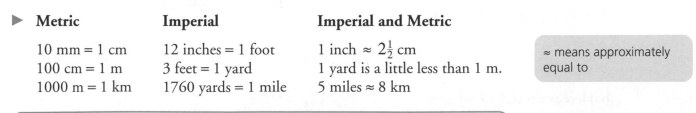

inches → × 2.54 → centimetres

....

a 4 × 2.54 = 10.16 cm
b Use the flow chart backwards, using inverse operations:

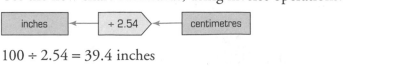

inches ← ÷ 2.54 ← centimetres

100 ÷ 2.54 = 39.4 inches

÷ is the inverse of ×
(see N8 for inverses).

Exercise S9

L3

1 Choose the correct answer from each list:

   a A tram is about _____ high.
    3 mm   3 cm   3 m   3 km.
   b A ruler is about _____ long.
    30 mm   30 cm   30 m   30 km.
   c A car is about _____ long.
    4 mm   4 cm   4 m   4 km.
   d The distance from Sheffield to Leeds is about _____.
    60 mm   60 cm   60 m   60 km.
   e A paper clip is about _____ long.
    30 mm   30 cm   30 m   30 km.

2 Give the most sensible metric unit to measure:

   a the distance from your school to centre of London.
   b the length of this book.
   c the height of a large tree.

L4

3 Use the flowchart to change these measurements to centimetres.

See N8 for inverse operations.

   a 10 mm
   b 100 mm
   c 1 m
   d 1.5 m
   e 1.05 m

4 In the 4 × 400 relay running race, 4 competitors each run 400 m.
What is the total distance run in:
   a m
   b km?

M **5** How many millimetres are there in one centimetre?

6 Three students measured their height.
Put them in order of size, smallest first.
Explain your reasoning.
Brett 147 cm
Jason 1.5 m
Kelly 1470 mm

L5

7 A standard imperial ruler is 12 inches long.
How long is this in centimetres?

8 It is 10 miles from Sheffield to Chesterfield.
How far is this in kilometres?

9 Is a mile more or less than a kilometre?

M **10** A window is one metre wide.
Approximately how many feet is this?

11 It is 640 km from Lisbon to Madrid.
How many miles is this?

S10 Mass and capacity

▶ **Mass** can be measured in metric or imperial units.

Metric units		
gram (g)	**kilogram (kg)**	

A grain of rice has a mass of about 1 g.

An apple has a mass of about 100 g.

A bag of sugar has a mass of 1 kg.

Imperial units	
ounce (oz)	**pound (lb)**

A tomato has a mass of about 1 oz.

A large jar of jam has a mass of 1 lb.

KEYWORDS

Mass	Millilitre
Gram	Centilitre
Kilogram	Litre
Ounce	Pint
Pound	Gallon
Capacity	

The different units of mass are related:

1000 g = 1 kg

16 oz = 1 lb

$\approx$ means approximately equal to.

1 oz $\approx$ 25 g
1 lb $\approx$ 450 g
1 kg $\approx$ 2.2 lb

example

Change these measurements to grams.

a 2 kg   **b** 2.5 kg   **c** 40 kg

....

As 1 kg = 1000 g, you multiply by 1000 to change kilograms to grams.

a $2 \times 1000 = 1000$ g
b $2.5 \times 1000 = 2500$ g
c $40 \times 1000 = 40\,000$ g

▶ **Capacity** can be measured in metric or imperial units.

Capacity is the amount of fluid a container will hold.

Metric units		
millilitre (ml)	**centilitre (cl)**	**litre (l)**

A teaspoon has a capacity of about 5 ml.

A coffee mug has a capacity of about 25 cl.

A milk carton has a mass of about 1 l.

Imperial units	
pint	**gallon**

A milk bottle has a capacity of 1 pint.

8 milk bottles have a capacity of 1 gallon.

example

Change these measurements to litres.

a 500 ml   **b** 75 cl   **c** 2500 ml

....

a 1000 ml = 1 l. Divide by 1000 to change millilitres to litres.
  $500 \div 1000 = 0.5$ l
b 100 cl = 1 l. Divide by 100 to change centilitres to litres.
  $75 \div 100 = 0.75$ l
c $2500 \div 1000 = 2.5$ l

The different units of capacity are related:
1000 ml = 1 l
100 cl = 1 l

8 pints = 1 gallon

1 pint $\approx$ 600 ml
1 gallon $\approx 4\frac{1}{2}$ l

62

Exercise S10

L3

1 Choose the correct answer.
A bag of sugar weighs _____.

    a 1 g   **b** 10 g   **c** 100 g   **d** 1 kg   **e** 10 kg

2 Choose the correct answer.
A bucket holds _____ of water.

    a 10 ml   **b** 10 cl   **c** 1 l   **d** 10 l   **e** 100 l

3 Choose the correct answer.
A small bottle holds _____ of drink.
    a 5 ml   **b** 50 ml   **c** 500 ml   **d** 5000 ml   **e** 50 000 ml

4 Give the most sensible metric unit to measure:
    a your weight
    b the capacity of a glass.

L4

5 A book weighs 500 g.
How many kilograms would 5 books weigh?

6 Use the flow chart to change:
    a 1 kg to pounds   **b** 11 lb to kilograms.

7 A can holds 330 ml of drink.
Do 3 cans hold more drink than a 1-litre bottle?
Explain your answer.

8 A small carton of yoghurt weighs 125 g.
Calculate the mass of a pack of 4 yoghurts in:

    a g   **b** kg

9 Change these measurements to millilitres.

    a 1 litre   **b** $2\frac{1}{2}$ litres   **c** 1 cl   **d** 10 cl   **e** 100 cl

10 Each glass holds 250 ml. How many full glasses can
you fill from a 2 l bottle of lemonade?

L5 **M**

11 How many millilitres is the same as one pint?
Choose the best answer:
    a 6 ml   **b** 60 ml   **c** 600 ml   **d** 6000 ml

M

12 Is a kilogram more or less than a pound?

13 There are 8 pints in a gallon.
Two pints is just more than a litre.
How many litres is approximately the same as one gallon?

M

14 Is one pint more or less than one litre?

▶ **Perimeter** is the distance around a shape.
It is the total length of the sides of a shape.

KEYWORDS
Perimeter   Surface area
Area   Volume
Perpendicular

example

Find the perimeter of these shapes.

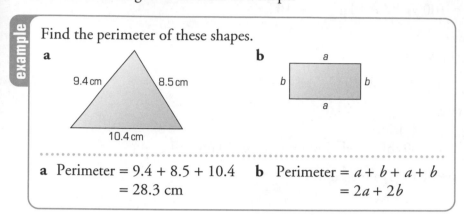

a

b

a Perimeter = 9.4 + 8.5 + 10.4   b Perimeter = $a + b + a + b$
              = 28.3 cm   = $2a + 2b$

▶ **Area** is the amount of space covered by a flat shape.

You can count squares to find the area of irregular shapes.

Areas of rectangles can be found using the formula:

▶ Area of a rectangle = length × width

Area is measured in squares, e.g. square centimetres.
Square centimetre is written as cm^2 for short.

example

Find the area of this shape.

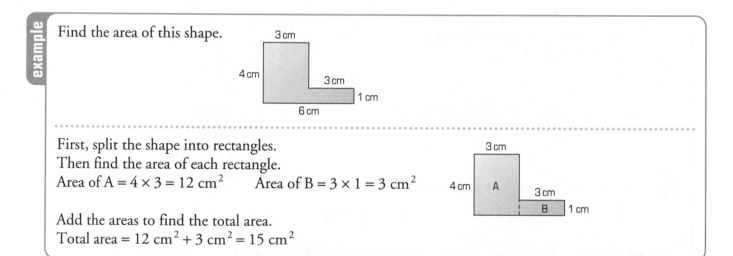

First, split the shape into rectangles.
Then find the area of each rectangle.
Area of A = 4 × 3 = 12 cm^2 Area of B = 3 × 1 = 3 cm^2

Add the areas to find the total area.
Total area = 12 cm^2 + 3 cm^2 = 15 cm^2

The area of a triangle is half the area of the surrounding rectangle.

▶ Area of a triangle = $\frac{1}{2}$ × base × height = $\frac{1}{2}$ × b × h

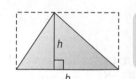

The base and height are perpendicular

▶ The **surface area** of a cuboid is found by adding the areas of the six faces.

The surface area of the cuboids is the same as the area of the net.

Surface area = (3 × 2) + (3 × 2) + (2 × 1) + (2 × 1) + (1 × 3) + (1 × 3)
             = 6 + 6 + 2 + 2 + 3 + 3
             = 22 cm^2

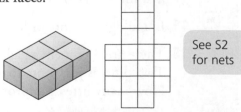

See S2 for nets

▶ **Volume** is the amount of space a solid shape takes up.

By counting cubes, the volume of this shape is 6 cm^3.

Volume is measured in cubes, e.g. cubic centimetres.
Cubic centimetre is written as cm^3 for short.

Exercise S11

1 What is the area of each of the shaded shapes?

a   b   c   d   e

2 What is the perimeter of the shaded shapes in question 1?

 3 What is the area of this square?

8 cm

4 How many cubes are needed to make each of these shapes?

a   b   c   d 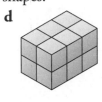   e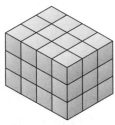

5 On a centimetre squared grid, draw a shape that has an area of 4 cm² and a perimeter of 10 cm.

6 A rectangle is divided into 8 triangles as shown.

    a Calculate the area of the large rectangle.
    b Calculate the area of one of the triangles.

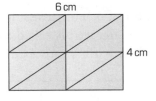

6 cm

4 cm

7 Calculate the perimeter of this rectangle.

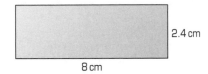

2.4 cm

8 cm

 8 What is the area of this triangle?

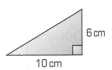

6 cm

10 cm

9 The perimeter of a square is 12 cm.
Calculate the area of the square.

 10 Calculate the surface area of these cuboids.

a   b   c   d 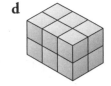   e

11 Calculate the area of these shapes.

a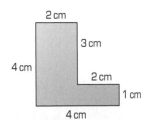

2 cm
3 cm
4 cm
2 cm
1 cm
4 cm

b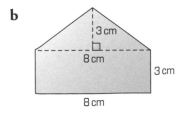

3 cm
8 cm
3 cm
8 cm

65

There are two types of data: **primary data** and **secondary data**.

▶ **Primary data** are data you collect yourself.

You can use a data collection sheet or frequency table.

You could record the number of packets of crisps eaten by students in your class yesterday in a table like this:

KEYWORDS
Data	Survey
Primary data	Questionnaire
Secondary data	Sample size
Data collection sheet	
Two-way table	

Number of packets	Tally	Frequency
0–2	卌 卌 卌 III	
3–5	卌 II	
6–8	IIII	
9+	I	

The intervals must not overlap.

The frequency is the total tally.
卌 means five students.

Primary data can also be collected in a **survey** using a **questionnaire**.

Questionnaires need to give reliable data.

▶ The questions should not be embarrassing or biased.
▶ The number of people surveyed is called the **sample size**.
▶ The larger the sample size, the more accurate the data will be.

example

A student stands by a vending machine and asks five girls and five boys in the queue, 'Do you like fizzy drinks?'
Give reasons why this is not a good survey.

	Yes	No
Boys	4	1
Girls	2	3

This grid is called a two-way table

2 girls liked fizzy drinks

The sample size is too small, 10 students is not enough.
The data will be biased. The students are in a vending machine queue.
The question is vague. There are many possible answers:
'depends which flavour',
'a bit',
'a lot'.
It is a good idea to give answer options.

▶ **Secondary data** are data that have already been collected.

You find secondary data in books, newspapers and on the internet.

The sample size was approximately 3000 for the data in the graph.

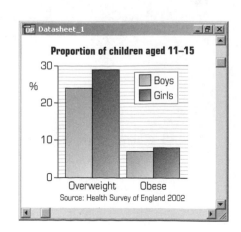

Exercise D1

L3

1 The survey results of a class are shown.
  a How many students are in the class?
  b How many are left-handed girls?
  c How many right-handed students are there?

	Number of boys	Number of girls
Left-handed	2	3
Right-handed	12	13

2 The average number of daily hours of sunshine are shown.
  a How many hours of sunshine should I expect on a July day in Malaga?
  b Which month has most sunshine in the Ardèche?
  c Which place has least sunshine in October?

	June	July	Aug	Sept	Oct
Ardèche	9.5	10	10.5	10	9
Malaga	10	11	12	11.5	10.5

L4

3 Jack wants to know whether more boys than girls in his class attend school. He asked, 'Were you ever absent from school last week?'

  a What labels are needed on the two-way table?
  b Jack then asked, 'How many times were you absent from school last week?' The results were:

  0 1 0 2 0 5
  1 1 0 0 0 4
  2 0 1 4 0 0
  0 0 0 5 0 10

  Tally these data into the grouped frequency table.

Number of absences	Tally	Frequency
0–2		
3–5		
6–8		
9+		

L5

4 Sarah wants to find out how often students in her year are given maths homework. She gives a questionnaire to five of her friends. One part of it is shown.

  a Give two reasons why the answer section is unsatisfactory
  b Suggest three new choices for the answer section.
  c Write one comment about the sample size.

Question: How often are you given maths homework?
Answer:
☐ Sometimes   ☐ Occasionally   ☐ Usually

5 A survey of vehicles takes place. Which data collection sheet is easier to use, A or B? Explain your reason.

  A Car, Car, Car, Van, Bus
  Van, Lorry, Bus, Car, Car
  Car, Van, Van, Car, Car

  B

Type of vehicle	Tally	Frequency
Car	⟋⟋⟋⟋ III	8
Van	IIII	4
Bus	II	2
Other	I	1

6 A test is marked out of 50. The teacher wants to put the results in a frequency table.

  a Explain what is wrong with the frequency table.
  b Draw a more suitable frequency table.

Mark	Tally	Frequency
0–10		
10–20		
20–30		
30–40		
40–50		

Calculating statistics

▶ An average is a single value that is typical of the data.

There are three different types of average: **mode**, **median** and **mean**.

▶ The **mode** is the value in the data that occurs most often:

The mode of 2, 2, 2, 3, 3, 4, 6, 7, 7 is 2 because it occurs most often: three times.

The modal colour in the table is blue as it occurs most often.

Colour	Frequency
Red	2
Blue	7
Yellow	0
Green	1

The mode can have more that one value.
For example, the mode of 2, 2, 3, 4, 4 is 2 and 4 because they both occur twice.

▶ The **modal group** or **modal class** is the group of data that occurs most often.

The modal group in the table is 46–50 as it occurs most often.

Weight (kg)	40–45	46–50	51–55	56–60
Frequency	3	4	2	1

▶ The **median** is the middle value when the data are put in order of size.

example

Find the median of these sets of data:

a 3, 2, 2, 3, 4, 6, 7, 2, 7   **b** 5, 4, 3, 4, 5, 6

a Arrange in order:
2, 2, 2, 3, 3, 4, 6, 7, 7

The median is 3 as the middle value is 3.

b Arrange in order:
3, 4, 4, 5, 5, 6

There are two middle numbers: 4 and 5.
The median is halfway: $4\frac{1}{2}$.

If there are two middle numbers, add them and divide by 2.

▶ The **mean** is the total divided by the number of values.

example

Find the mean of these numbers:
2, 5, 2, 3, 8

The total is 2 + 5 + 2 + 3 + 8 = 20. There are five values.
The mean = 20 ÷ 5 = 4

The mean is what most people call the average.

▶ The **range** is a measure that describes how the data is spread out.
Range = highest value − lowest value

The range of 3, 3, 4, 4, 8, 8, 9, 10 is 10 − 3 = 7.

example

Choose four numbers so that the mean is 5 and the range is 7.

If the mean is 5, the total of all the numbers = 5 × 4 = 20.
Highest number − lowest number = 7.

One possible answer is: 1, 3, 8 and 8.

Check:
1 + 3 + 8 + 8 = 20.   8 − 1 = 7

Exercise D2

1 Here are 10 numbers: 6, 7, 7, 8, 4, 4, 8, 4, 7, 5.

  a Find the mode.
  b Calculate the range.

2 Jack was the modal boy's name and Emily was the modal girl's name
for babies born in 2003.
Explain what this means.

3 Chloe's lowest exam mark was 45%. Her range was 20%.
What was her highest mark?

 4 Find the mean of 3, 6 and 6.

5 Here are 7 numbers: 0, 4, 4, 6, 7, 7, 7.

  a Calculate the mean.
  b Work out the median.

6 The numbers of students in height groups
are shown in the bar chart.
What is the modal group?

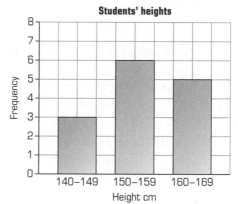

7 Here are 10 numbers: 8, 3, 2, 7, 8, 9, 7, 4, 5, 1.

  a Find the mode.
  b Calculate the range.
  c Calculate the mean.
  d Work out the median.

8 Here is a box of matches.
In 10 boxes of matches, the number of
matches in each box were:
37, 45, 41, 41, 42, 44, 39, 40, 41, 40

  a Find the mean number of matches per box.
  b The box states, 'Average contents 40.'
    Is this statement accurate? Give a reason for your answer.

9 Choose 3 numbers so that the range is 2,
and the mean is 4.

10 Write down 3 different numbers that have a mean of 5.

11 The graph shows the number of chocolate
sweets in 10 packets.
  a What is the modal number of sweets?
  b Calculate the range of the number of sweets.

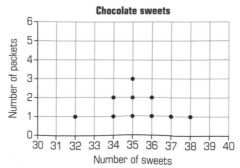

L3

1 Liam did a survey of the eye colour of all the children in his class.
This table shows his results:

	Number of Boys	Number of Girls
Brown eyes	11	12
Blue eyes	4	3

a How many children are there in Liam's class?

b How many children in Liam's class have brown eyes?

c Two new children join Liam's class.
They are both boys.
One has brown eyes and the other has blue eyes.
Liam changes the numbers in his table.
Copy and complete the table for Liam's class now.

d Julie does a survey of 10 children in her class.
She records her results like this:

Boy or girl	Boy	Girl	Boy	Girl	Girl	Boy	Girl	Boy	Girl	Boy
Colour of eyes	Brown	Brown	Blue	Blue	Brown	Brown	Brown	Brown	Blue	Brown

Copy and complete the table from part **c** again, to show Julie's results:

e There are 14 boys and 17 girls in Mari's class.
10 boys and 13 girls have brown eyes. The others have blue eyes.
Copy the table again.
Use the information to complete it for Mari's class.

(D1)

2 In each part, write the letter of the statement which is most likely to be true.

a
A | The kettle in my kitchen holds 2 litres of water.
B | The kettle in my kitchen holds 20 litres of water.
C | The kettle in my kitchen holds 200 litres of water.
D | The kettle in my kitchen holds 2000 litres of water.

b
A | The door to my room is 2 mm high.
B | The door to my room is 2 cm high.
C | The door to my room is 2 m high.
D | The door to my room is 2 km high.

c
A | The apple in my bag weighs 1 gram.
B | The apple in my bag weighs 10 grams.
C | The apple in my bag weighs 100 grams.
D | The apple in my bag weighs 1000 grams.

(S9)

(S10)

M

3 It takes three hours to travel from my home to my friend's house.
I arrive at two pm.
At what time did I leave home? Write your answer using am or pm.

(S8)

L4

4 a Lisa works in a shoe shop.
She recorded the size of each pair of trainers that
she sold during a week.
The table shows what she wrote down.
Use a tallying method to make a table showing how
many pairs of trainers of each size were sold during
the whole week.

	Size of trainers sold					
Monday	7	7	5	6		
Tuesday	6	4	4	8		
Wednesday	5	8	6	7	5	
Thursday	7	4	5			
Friday	7	4	9	5	7	8
Saturday	6	5	7	6	9	4	7

b Which size of trainer did Lisa sell the most?

c Lisa said, 'Most of the trainers sold were bigger than size 6.'
How can you tell from your table that Lisa is wrong?

(D1)

(D2)

L4 Ⓜ **5** How many centimetres are there in one metre?

6 a Write how many small cubes there are in this cuboid.

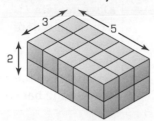

b This shape is made with two cuboids.
Write how many small cubes there are
in this shape.

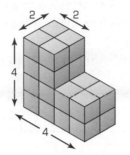

Ⓜ **7** Centimetres are a measure of length.
Copy and complete the sentence: Grams are a measure of ...

L5 **8** Hannah went on a cycling holiday.
The table shows how far she cycled each day.
Hannah says:
   'On average, I cycled over 40 km a day'.
Show that Hannah is wrong.

Monday	32.3 km
Tuesday	38.7 km
Wednesday	43.5 km
Thursday	45.1 km

9 a There are four people in Sita's family.
Their shoe sizes are 4, 5, 7 and 10
What is the median shoe size in Sita's family?
b There are three people in John's family.
The range of their shoe sizes is 4.
Two people in the family wear shoe size 6
John's shoe size is not 6 and it is not 10.
What is John's shoe size?

10 A scale measures in grams and in ounces.

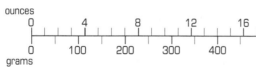

Use the scale to answer these questions.
a About how many ounces is 400 grams?
b About how many grams is 8 ounces?
c About how many ounces is 1 kilogram?
Explain your answer.

11 a Which of the rectangles below have an area of 12 cm²?

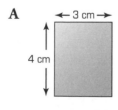 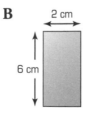 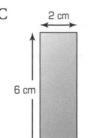 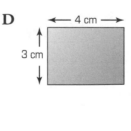

b A square has an area of 100 cm²
What is its perimeter? Show your working.

S9
S11
S10
D2
D2
S10
S9

71

▶ **Discrete data** can be counted.
The data can only have particular values such as the
number of packets of crisps or number of cars.

▶ **Continuous data** can take any value in a range.
It is usually a measure such as mass or length.

▶ **Pictograms** display data using pictures to represent frequencies.

These are the results
from Sarah's music
collection.

Type	Frequency
Rock	8
Pop	2
Rap	6

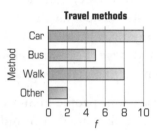

You need to use
a key

▶ **Bar charts** display data using bars to represent frequencies.

Tom's class were asked,
'How did you travel to
school today?'

Method	Frequency
Car	10
Bus	5
Walk	8
Other	2

Travel methods

Car is the mode.

▶ **Bar-line graphs** display data using lines to represent frequencies.

A dice was rolled
40 times and
the scores were recorded.

Score	1	2	3	4	5	6
Frequency	6	8	5	10	6	5

The mode is 4.

Dice scores

▶ **Comparative bar charts** display two sets of data on the same bar chart.

The table shows the
number of merits given
out to students in Toni's
class.

	Autumn	Spring	Summer
Boys	15	10	15
Girls	20	12	17

▶ **Percentage bar charts** display data on a bar. The length of the bar represents 100%.

Here are the 2001 UK
Census results for age.

Below 16	16 and above
20%	80%

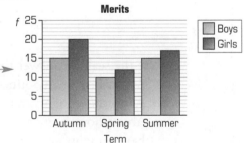

▶ **Pie charts** display data using angles to represent frequencies.

These results show the
favourite crisp flavours of
eight students.

Flavour	Frequency
Plain	5
Salt and vinegar	2
Cheese and onion	1

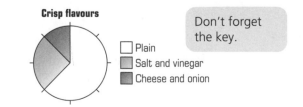

Don't forget
the key.

Exercise D3

L3

1 Sally asked her class, 'Do you have a pet?'
10 students said yes.
15 students said no.
Copy and complete the pictogram to show this information.

Key: 😊 represents 5 students

Yes	😊 😊
No	

2 Twenty people were asked to name their favourite drink.
Draw a pictogram to illustrate this information.
Use 🥤 to represent 2 people.

Drink	Tally	Frequency
Tea	卌 III	8
Coffee	IIII	4
Lemonade	III	3
Coke	卌	5

L4

3 30 students are asked to name their favourite fruit.

Fruit	Tally	Frequency
Apple	卌 卌	10
Banana	卌 卌 卌	15
Orange	卌	5

Show this information in a pie chart.

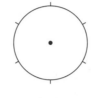

4 a Draw a bar chart for this frequency distribution.

Yellow cards	0–4	5–9	10–14	15–19
Frequency	5	4	10	6

b What is the modal number of yellow cards?

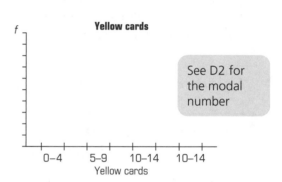

See D2 for the modal number

5 The vowels on a page of a book are counted. These are the results.

Vowel	a	e	i	o	u
f	12	18	16	15	4

a Draw a bar-line graph to show this information.
b Which letter is the mode?

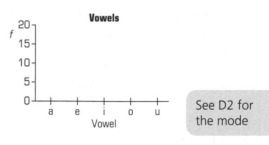

See D2 for the mode

L5

6 Mike's table tennis team have these results:
Won   60%
Drawn   15%
Lost   25%
Copy and complete the percentage bar chart to illustrate these results.

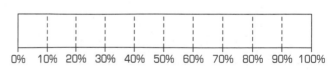

7 An average adult spends a typical day as shown.
Draw a bar chart to show this information.

Activity	Hours
Sleeping	8
Eating	1
Working	8
Watching TV	2
Other	5

Source: UK 2000 Time-use Survey
Office for National Statistics

8 Shamina asked her class how they travelled to school. The results are shown in the table.

a Draw a comparative bar chart to show these results.
b How many students are in Shaminas's class?

	Car	Bus	Walk
Boys	8	4	1
Girls	10	6	0

See D1 for two-way tables

73

You need to be able to read information from graphs and charts.
Remember to read the key carefully.

▶ You can extract information from **pictograms**.

> **example**
>
> This pictogram shows the hours of TV watched in one week by a group of students.
>
> a What does ☐ represent?
> b How many hours did each student watch?
> c Find the total number of hours watched.
> d Which student probably does not have a TV?
>
> ☐ represents 4 hours
>
> | Jo | ☐ ☐ ☐ ☐ |
> | Luke | ☐ ☐ ☐ ▯ |
> | Ryan | |
> | Matthew | ☐ ☐ ▯ |
>
> ....
>
> a ☐ is $\frac{1}{2}$ of ☐
> $\frac{1}{2}$ of 4 hours = 2 hours
> b Jo: $4 \times 4 = 16$ hours   Luke: $3\frac{1}{2} \times 4 = 14$ hours
>   Ryan: $0 \times 4 = 0$ hours   Matthew: $2\frac{1}{2} \times 4 = 10$ hours
> c $16 + 14 + 0 + 10 = 40$ hours
> d Ryan (he didn't watch any TV)

▶ A **pie chart** uses a circle split into sectors to display data.

> **example**
>
> Twelve students are asked to choose their favourite sport.
> The pie chart shows the information.
>
> a Calculate the angle for football.
> b How many students chose football?
> c How many more students chose ice hockey than basketball?
>
>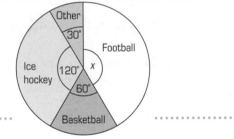
>
> ....
>
> a The angles at a point add to 360°.
> $x + 30 + 60 + 120 = 360$
> $x + 210 = 360°$
> $x = 150°$
> b The whole circle (360°) represents 12 students.
>   So 1 student is represented by $360 \div 12 = 30°$.
> $150° \div 30° = 5$, so 5 students chose football.
> c $4 \times 30° = 120°$ and so 4 chose ice hockey
> $2 \times 30° = 60$ and so 2 chose basketball
>   So $4 - 2 = 2$ more students.
>
> **Check:**
> Ice hockey is twice as big as
> basketball on the pie chart.

▶ **Line graphs** show how data changes over a period of time.

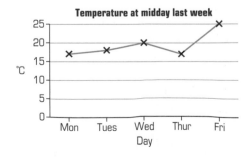

Mean temperature = $(17 + 18 + 20 + 17 + 25) \div 5$
$= 97 \div 5$
$= 19.4\,°C$

See D2 for the mean

The **trend** is generally upward during the week – it is getting warmer.

Exercise D4

L3

1 The pictogram shows the number of houses for sale on 4 roads in a new housing estate.

    a Which road has the lowest number of houses for sale?
    b How many houses are for sale on The Green?
    c How many houses are for sale on the whole estate?

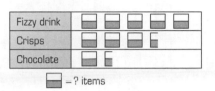

= 10 houses

2 The pictogram shows 20 items that were sold from a vending machine.

    a What does ☐ represent?
    b How many fizzy drinks were sold?
    c How many packets of crisps were sold?

= ? items

M

3 In a pictogram 🕴 represents 50 people.
What would 🕴 represent?

L4

4 A dice is thrown 36 times.
The pie chart shows the results.

    a Calculate the missing angle.
    b How many times was 1 scored?
    c Do you think the dice is fair?
       Explain your answer.

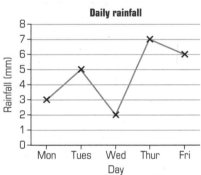

Dice scores

5 The graph shows the rainfall in mm for 5 successive days.

    a Calculate the total rainfall over the 5 days.
    b Which day had the most rain?

Daily rainfall

M

6 The pie chart shows the proportion of students who do not eat breakfast.
What percentage of students do eat breakfast?

L5 **M**

7 The proportion of male and female teachers is shown in this pie chart.

    a What percentage of teachers are female?
    b If there are 75 teachers altogether, how many male and how many female teachers are there?

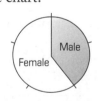

See N6 for percentages.

8 Allan asked each students in his class for their favourite flavour of crisp.
The results are shown in the pie chart.
Eight students chose plain.
How many students are there in Allan's class?

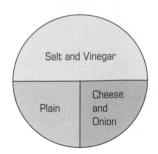

▶ The lengths of the bars in a **bar chart** represent the frequencies.

The chart shows the number of students from each year in a quiz.

KEYWORDS
Bar chart   Bar line graph
Grouped data
Percentage bar chart

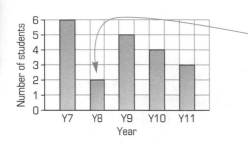

Year 8 has the lowest bar.
This represents 2 students.

The total number of students is
6 + 2 + 5 + 4 + 3 = 20 students.

▶ The lengths of the lines in a **bar-line graph** represent the frequencies.

The graph shows the scores for 9 holes of golf.

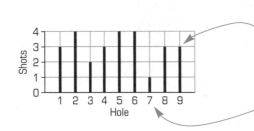

3 shots were taken on hole 9.

A hole-in-one was scored on
hole 7.

Mean number of shots =
Total ÷ number of holes
Total = 3 + 4 + 2 + 3 + 4 + 4 + 1 + 3 + 3
    = 27
Mean = 27 ÷ 9 = 3

See D2 for the mean

▶ Some bar charts show **grouped data**.

This chart shows the number of people from each age group
that take part in a sport or physical activity.

The chart shows that:

▷ The age group 8–15 years is the most active.
▷ The least active group is 65 and over.
▷ The older you are the less exercise you do.

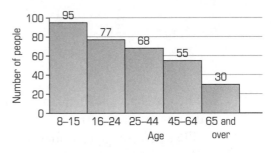

Source: UK 2000 Time use Survey
Office for National Satistics

▶ The percentages in a **percentage bar chart** add up to 100%.

The chart shows what 200 students do for lunch.

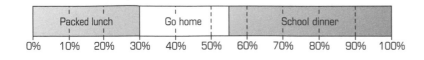

See N6 for percentages

The chart shows that:

▷ 55% – 30% = 25% go home for lunch.
▷ School dinner is the modal lunch arrangement (it is the largest).
▷ 30% of 200 = 60 students have a packed lunch.
▷ 45% of 200 = 90 students have a school dinner.

30% means 3 × 10%
10% of 200 = 20
so   30% of 200 = 60

Exercise D5

L3 **M** **1** The bar chart shows the number of people who voted yes, no or don't know in a survey. How many people voted?

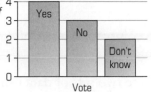

2 Jaya asks her class to give the reason why they last used a computer. The results are shown.

a What is the modal result?
b What is the least popular reason?
c How many students used the internet?
d How many students are there in Jaya's class?

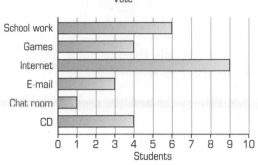

3 The results of a football team are shown on the graph.

a How many games have been won?
b How many games have been played?
c What is the probability that the next game will be a draw?

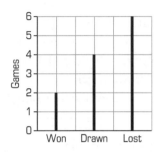

L4 **M** **4** The chart shows the percentage of votes cast. What percentage voted No?

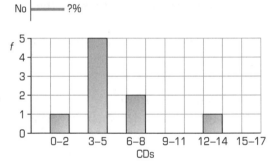

5 The bar chart shows the number of CDs bought by Megan and her friends in one year. How many people are shown in the chart?

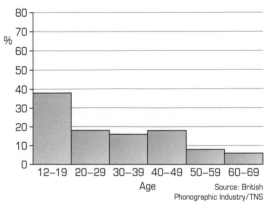

6 The graph shows the percentage of each age group that bought at least one music single in 2002.

a What is the modal age group?
b Explain why it is not possible to calculate the range of the ages.

> See D2 for the modal group and range

L5 **7** A card is taken out of a pack and the suit is recorded.

| Hearts | Clubs | Diamonds | Spades |

0% 10% 20% 30% 40% 50% 60% 70% 80% 90% 100%

> See N6 for percentages

a What percentage of the cards were Diamonds?
b If 20 cards were taken out altogether how many were:
  i Hearts   ii Clubs
  iii Diamonds   iv Spades?

You often need to compare two sets of data.

▶ You can compare two sets of data using the **mode**, **median**, **mean** and **range**.

example

Ewan and Mia did five mental tests. Here are their scores.

Ewan: 2, 3, 3, 5, 9
Mia: 3, 4, 4, 5, 6

a Find the mean and the range for each student.
b Who achieved the better marks?
c Who is more consistent?

a Ewan: mean = (2 + 3 + 3 + 5 + 9) ÷ 5 = 4.4
            range = 9 − 2 = 7
   Mia: mean = (3 + 4 + 4 + 5 + 6) ÷ 5 = 4.4
            range = 6 − 3 = 3
b The means are identical.
c Mia is more consistent as her range is smaller.

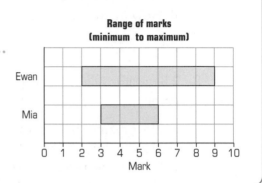

Range of marks (minimum to maximum)

You can also use graphs to compare data.

▶ **Line graphs** can display more than one set of data at the same time.

The average monthly temperature is shown for Fuerteventura and Biarritz.

The temperature is more consistent in Fuerteventura. Each month, it is colder in Biarritz than in Fuerteventura.

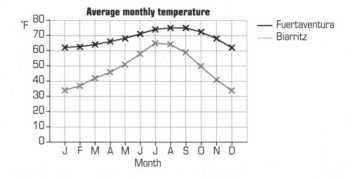

Average monthly temperature
— Fuerteventura
— Biarritz

▶ **Comparative bar charts** help you to compare different sets of data.

The chart shows the percentages of males and females who read a newspaper, magazines or fiction book last week.

▷ More females read fiction books than males.
▷ Over 80% of males and females read a newspaper last week.

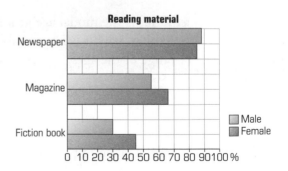

Reading material
■ Male
■ Female

▶ To compare **pie charts** you need to know the total frequency for each chart.

8 boys and 12 girls were asked if they like cola.
The results are shown in the pie charts.

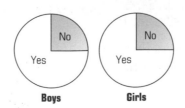

Boys   Girls

$\frac{1}{4}$ of the boys said no.
$\frac{1}{4}$ of 8 = 2 boys.
$\frac{1}{4}$ of girls said no.
$\frac{1}{4}$ of 12 = 3 girls.
More girls than boys said no.

Exercise D6

1 The bar chart shows the test results for a class. How many students passed in total?

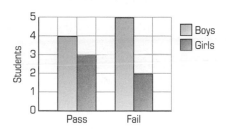

2 10 girls and 20 boys were asked to name their favourite lesson. The results are shown in the pie charts.

  a What is the favourite lesson for the girls?
  b Calculate the number of boys who like English most.
  c Ross said, 'The number of boys who like maths is the same as the number of girls who like maths.' Explain if he is correct.

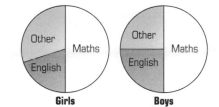

3 The chart shows the average daily distance walked by different age groups in 1985 and 2000.

  a How far did the under 10s walk each day in 1985?
  b How far did the 10–19s walk each day in 2000?
  c What do you think the graph shows?

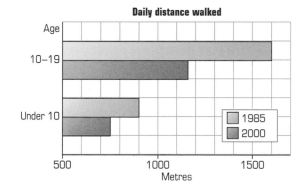

4 10 girls and 8 boys take a test.
The results are shown on the graphs.

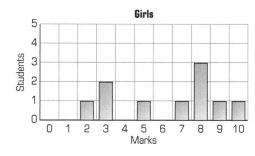
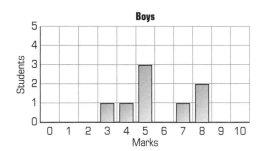

  a List all the marks for the girls.
  b Calculate the mean and range for the girls.
  c List all the marks for the boys.
  d Calculate the mean and the range for the boys.
  e What do the means tell you about the girls' and boys' abilities?
  f What do the ranges tell you about the girls' and boys' abilities?

See D2 for mean and range

5 The graph shows the hours of daylight for four months in London.
For example, in January the hours of daylight range from 0800 to 1600.

  a What is the latest time daylight finishes in February.
  b Which month has the longest hours of daylight?

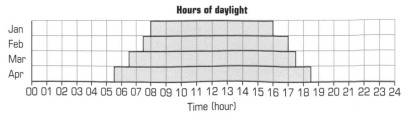

These words describe the likelihood of an event happening.

| Impossible | Unlikely | Even chance | Likely | Certain |

You can describe likelihood using numbers called probabilities.

▶ **Probability** measures the likelihood of something happening.

You can write probabilities as fractions, decimals and percentages:

Impossible   Certain

| 0 | $\frac{1}{10}$ | $\frac{2}{10}$ | $\frac{3}{10}$ | $\frac{4}{10}$ | $\frac{5}{10}$ | $\frac{6}{10}$ | $\frac{7}{10}$ | $\frac{8}{10}$ | $\frac{9}{10}$ | 1 |

| 0 | 0.1 | 0.2 | 0.3 | 0.4 | 0.5 | 0.6 | 0.7 | 0.8 | 0.9 | 1 |

| 0% | 10% | 20% | 30% | 40% | 50% | 60% | 70% | 80% | 90% | 100% |

Look back to N6 to remind yourself of these equivalences.

example

A card is picked out of a pack of 52 playing cards.
Half the cards are red, and half are black.
What is the probability that the card is:

a red   **b** blue   **c** red or black?

....

a Half the cards are red so the probability is $\frac{1}{2}$.
You can also write 0.5 or 50%.
b None of the cards are blue so the probability is 0.
It is impossible.
c All the cards are either red or black so the probability is 1.
It is certain.

You can find the probability of an event not happening.

An event either happens or it doesn't.

▶ Probability of an event happening + probability of event not happening = 1.

example

The probability that Kai will catch the ball is 0.7.

What is the probability that he will not catch the ball?

....

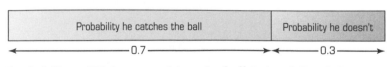

Probability of Kai not catching the ball is 1 − 0.7 = 0.3.

Check
0.3 + 0.7 = 1

example

When a coin is tossed, it will be a Head or a Tail.
The probability it will be a Head is 0.5.
What is the probability it will be a Tail?

....

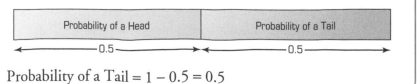

Probability of a Tail = 1 − 0.5 = 0.5

If the probability of a Head is not 0.5 then the coin is unfair or biased.

Check:
0.5 + 0.5 = 1

Exercise D7

M **1** What is the probability of an event that is impossible?

2 There are 8 coloured balls in a bag:
4 blue, 2 black and 2 white.

Dave takes a ball from the bag without looking.

a Which colour is he most likely to pick? Explain why.
b Which colours are equally likely to be picked? Explain why.

3 **a** Match these events with how likely they are to happen.

It will be windy every day for a month.		unlikely
A baby girl will be born somewhere in the world tomorrow.		likely
A man will walk on Jupiter tomorrow.		certain
It will be sunny sometime in the next week.		impossible

b Mark the events on a probability scale like this one:

impossible ⊢————————————————————————————⊣ certain

L4 M **4** The probability that a student will be present at school is 0.9.
What is the probability that a student will be absent?

5 What is the probability of the arrow landing on blue for each spinner?

a   **b**   **c**   **d**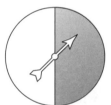

6 A fair coin is tossed 500 times.
How many times would you expect the outcome to be a Head.

L5 **7** This is part of a board game. It has 100 squares.
Some are blue, some are black.
Counters are thrown on the board.
The probability of landing on a blue square is $\frac{3}{10}$.
a What is the probability of landing on a black square?
b How many blue squares are there?
c How many black squares are there?

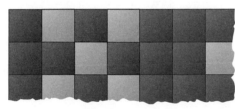

8 There are four DVDs on the shelf.
One is a romantic film, one is a cartoon, one is comedy and one is music.
Sinead picks a DVD from the shelf without looking.

a Sinead only likes comedy films.

Draw an arrow on a copy of the scale to show the probability
that Sinead will get a DVD she likes.

Probability that John
gets a DVD he likes

b How many types of DVD does John like?

▶ The **outcome** of an event is the result of a trial or experiment.

When you flip a coin there are two possible outcomes:
Heads and Tails.

KEYWORDS
Probability   Sample space
Outcome   Experiment
Event

▶ The probability of an event happening $= \dfrac{\text{number of those events}}{\text{number of possible events}}$

example

a   List the possible outcomes when throwing a dice.
b   Calculate the probability of throwing:
   i   a 6   ii   an even number   iii   a square number

····································

a   The 6 possible outcomes are 1, 2, 3, 4, 5, 6.
b   i   Probability of a $6 = \frac{1}{6}$

   ii   There are 3 even numbers on a dice.

   So the probability of getting an even number $= \frac{3}{6} = \frac{1}{2}$
   iii There are 2 square numbers.

   So the probability of getting a square number $= \frac{2}{6} = \frac{1}{3}$

See N5 for cancelling fractions

▶ A **sample space** diagram shows the possible outcomes of two successive events.

example

A mother gives birth to twins.
Show the possible outcomes in a sample space diagram.

··

		Born second	
		Boy	Girl
Born first	Boy	B, B	B, G
	Girl	G, B	G, G

Boy, Girl and Girl, Boy are not the same. The babies are born in a different order.

▶ You can estimate probabilities from an **experiment**.

example

A bag contains 20 cubes. The cubes are red, yellow, or green.
One cube is taken out, its colour is noted, and then it is replaced.
The results are shown in the table.

Colour	Frequency
Red	5
Yellow	3
Green	2

a   How many times was a cube taken out of the bag?
b   How many yellow cubes do you think are in the bag?
c   Estimate the probability of picking a green cube.

··

a   5 + 3 + 2 = 10 times
b   There were 3 yellow cubes when 10 cubes were taken out.
    So there could be 6 yellow cubes for 20 cubes.
c   2 green cubes were chosen out of the 10 times a cube was picked.
    So the probability $= \frac{2}{10} = \frac{1}{5}$.

Exercise D8

L3 **1** Ten cards numbered from 1 to 10 are placed face down.

A card is turned over. It is a 6. Another card is turned over.
Do you think the second card will be higher or lower?
Explain your reasoning.

M **2** What is the probability a coin will land on a head?

M **3** What is the probability of the spinner landing on a prime
number with this spinner?

See N3 for prime numbers

L4 **4** The letters in the word MATHEMATICS are placed in a box.
A letter is taken out at random.
What is the probability that it is a:

  a letter S
  b letter T
  c a vowel
  d a consonant?

5 The local take-away offers two meals for the price of one meal.
The meals must be chosen from pizza, burger or kebab.
List the possible combinations of two meals.

2 meals for the price of 1

6 A blue dice and a black dice are thrown and their scores
are added.

  a Copy and complete this sample space diagram.
  b What is the most likely total?
  c How many outcomes are there?

What is the probability of:

  d a 3
  e a multiple of 5
  f a total of more than 8?

Black dice

	•	••	•••	••••	•••••	••••••
•	2	3				
••	3	4				
•••						
••••						
•••••						
••••••						

Blue dice

M **7** There are 20 sweets left in a packet.
The table shows the colours of the sweets.
Ian picks a sweet at random.
What is the probability that the sweet is yellow?

Colour	f
Red	8
Yellow	5
Green	7

L5 **8** A jar contains lots of blue counters and lots of white counters.
Sian says, 'The probability of picking a white counter is $\frac{1}{2}$.'
Louis says, 'We don't have enough information to say what the
probability is.'
Who is right and why?

9 A giant pack of yoghurt contains 12 individual cartons.
Emily chooses a carton at random.
The table shows the probability of choosing each flavour.
Calculate how many cartons of
each flavour are in the 12-pack.

Flavour	Probability	Number of cartons
Vanilla	$\frac{1}{2}$	
Cherry	$\frac{1}{3}$	
Raspberry	$\frac{1}{6}$	

See N5 for fractions

L3

1 Amy and Ben do a survey together. They each draw a pictogram.

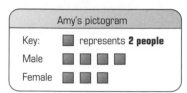

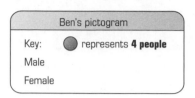

Ben shows the same information but uses a different key.
Copy and complete Ben's pictogram.

D3 D5

2 Here are some counters.
Some of them are circles, some are squares, and some are triangles.

Colin puts these **7** counters into a bag:

He takes one counter from his bag without looking.

a List all the shapes Colin could get when he takes one counter from his bag.
You can write or draw your answer.

b Which shape is Colin most likely to get? Explain your answer.

c Dilys wants to put some counters into another bag.
She wants to make it less likely that she will pick a square than a circle.
What counters could Dilys put into her bag?
You can write or draw your answer.

d Dele has got these counters in his bag: ● ■ ■ ▲ ▲ ▲
He wants to put some more counters in, to make it equally likely
that he will pick a square, circle or triangle.
What extra counters should Dele put into his bag?
You can write or draw your answer.

D7

L4

3 A teacher has five number cards. She says:

'I am going to take a card at random.
Each card shows a different positive whole number.
It is certain that the card will show a number less than 10
It is impossible that the card will show an even number.'

What numbers are on the cards?

D7

 4 Jim, Bob, Liz and Meg had a games competition.
They played two games, Draughts and Ludo.
Each pupil played each of the others at the two different games.

Meg recorded how many
games each person won.

Jim	III
Meg	III
Liz	IIII
Bob	II

Jim recorded who
won each game.

Draughts	Ludo
Jim	Meg
Liz	Bob
Bob	
Jim	Meg
Jim	Liz
Liz	Meg

D3 D4

a Jim forgot to put one of the names on his table.
Use Meg's table to work out what the missing name is.

b Who won the most games of Draughts?

c Give one reason why Meg's table is a good way of recording the results.

d Give one reason why Jim's table is a good way of recording the results.

5 A fair spinner has eight equal sections with a number on each section.
Five of them are even numbers. Three are odd numbers.
What is the probability that I spin an even number?

6 A newspaper predicts what the ages of secondary
school teachers will be in six years' time.
They print this chart.

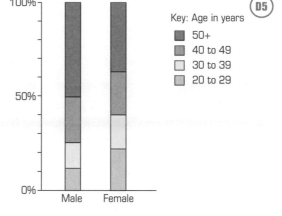

Key: Age in years
- 50+
- 40 to 49
- 30 to 39
- 20 to 29

a The chart shows 24% of male teachers will be
aged 40 to 49
About what percentage of female teachers will
be aged 40 to 49?

b About what percentage of female teachers will
be aged 50 +?

c The newspaper predicts there will be about
20 000 male teachers aged 40 to 49
Estimate the number of male teachers that
will be aged 50+.

d Assume the total number of male teachers will be about the same as the
total number of female teachers.
Use the chart to decide which statement is correct.
 A Generally, male teachers will tend to be younger than female teachers.
 B Generally, female teachers will tend to be younger than male teachers.
Explain how you used the chart to decide.

7 Les, Tom, Nia and Ann are in a singing competition.
To decide the order in which they will sing all four names are put into a bag.
Each name is taken out of the bag, one at a time, without looking.
a Write down all the possible orders with Tom singing second.
b In a different competition there are 8 singers.
The probability that Tom sings second is $\frac{1}{8}$.
Work out the probability that Tom does not sing second.

8 This graph shows the range in the temperature in Miami each month.
For example, in January the temperature ranges from 17 °C to 24 °C

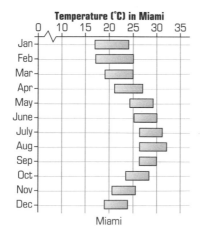

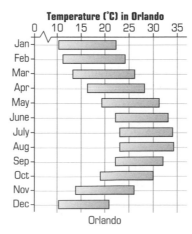

a In which month does Miami have the smallest range in temperature?
b In July, the range in the temperature in Miami is 5°
There are five other months in which the range in the temperature is 5°
Which five months are they?
c This graph shows the range in the temperature in Orlando each month.
In which three months is the maximum temperature in Miami greater
than the maximum temperature in Orlando?

Practice Test Paper 1: calculator not allowed   Levels 3–5

This test is 1 hour long.

You **must not** use a calculator for any question in this test.

You will need: pen, pencil, rubber, ruler, protractor, compasses, paper and graph paper.

1 These items were bought from a school vending machine:

	Crisps	Chocolate Bar	Apple	Fizzy drink	Bottled water
Boys	卅 III	卅 卅 II	II	卅 IIII	III
Girls	卅	卅 III	I	I	卅 II

  a How many boys bought a chocolate bar?

  b How many students bought a fizzy drink?

  c How many more girls than boys bought bottled water?   (3 *marks*)

2 a Add together 482 and 259.

  b Subtract 158 from 420.

  c Multiply 56 by 4.

  d Divide 245 by 5.   (4 *marks*)

3 There are six different ways to multiply three numbers to give 24.

Two have been done for you.

2 × 2 × 6 = 24		
1 × 3 × 8 = 24		
×	×	= 24
×	×	= 24
×	×	= 24
×	×	= 24

You can only use each set of numbers once.

Copy and complete the table.   (2 *marks*)

4 A chocolate bar has 12 pieces.

Jack, Gill and Jenny share the chocolate.

Jack has $\frac{1}{2}$ of the chocolate bar.

Gill has $\frac{1}{4}$ of the chocolate bar.

Jenny has whatever is left.

  a How many pieces does Jack have?

  b How many pieces does Gill have?

  c How many pieces does Jenny have?   (4 *marks*)

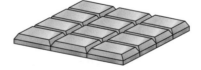

5 In a game, I roll five balls into numbered boxes.

The first four balls are shown.

  a What is the total score after four balls?

  b What is the highest total score I could
     get after I roll the fifth ball?   (3 *marks*)

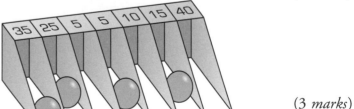

6 Copy this thermometer and mark on the scale.

  a Mark the position of 18 °C.

  b Mark the position of ⁻3 °C.

  c How many degrees warmer is 18 °C than ⁻3 °C?   (3 *marks*)

7 a Write two words from the list that describe the blue triangle:
   right angled
   scalene
   isosceles
   equilateral

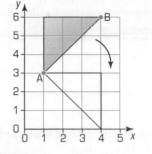

  b Write the coordinates of the point B.
  c The blue triangle is rotated about point A.
  Give the coordinates of the point that B moves to.   (4 *marks*)

8 The length of a car and trailer is 6.3 m.
   The car's length is 3.8 m.
   Find the length of the trailer.   (2 *marks*)

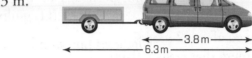

9 a Choose one word from the list to describe the blue angle:
   acute
   right angle
   obtuse
   reflex

  b Measure the blue angle.
  c Draw an angle of 48°.   (3 *marks*)

10 Alex has a 1 litre bottle of lemonade.
   A glass holds 250 ml.
   How many glasses will Alex be able to fill?   (2 *marks*)

11 The diagram shows a square and a rectangle.
   Write and simplify an expression for the perimeter of each shape.

                                                                             (2 *marks*)

12 a Calculate   **i** $4 \times 5 + 3$
                    ii $4 + 5 \times 3$

  b Write the calculation with brackets in to make the answer 32:

   $4 \times 5 + 3 = 32$ (3 *marks*)

13 a Choose the two nets that make a tetrahedron:
   A   **C**

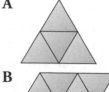

   B   **D**

  b Construct an equilateral triangle with sides of 6 cm,
  using compasses and ruler only.

                                                                             (4 *marks*)

14 Use this percentage reckoner to calculate VAT at $17\frac{1}{2}$%.

	£10	£20	£30	£40	£50
10%	£1	£2	£3	£4	£5
5%	50p	£1	£1.50	£2	£2.50
$2\frac{1}{2}$%	25p	50p	75p	£1	£1.25

Value Added Tax (VAT)
Ready Reckoner

  a Calculate $17\frac{1}{2}$% of £40.
  b The VAT is £3.50. What was the amount?
  c Calculate $17\frac{1}{2}$% of £60.   (6 *marks*)

15 a Each week I save £1.35.
     How much will I have saved after 52 weeks?
  b I want to buy a digital camera that costs £91.00.

     How much do I need to save each week, if I save £91 over 52 weeks?   (4 *marks*)

16 Solve the equations:
  a $7k + 2 = 16$
  b $2m - 1 = 8$ (2 *marks*)

17 Choose 3 different numbers from:

so that the median is 4 and the range is 3.   (2 *marks*)

18 A fair spinner has 5 sides. Each side has a number.
There are 2 even numbers and 3 odd numbers.
  a What is the probability it will land on an odd number?
     Give your answer as a fraction.
  b Mark the probability of an odd number on a copy of this probability scale:

       0 ————————————————————— 1

  c Express this probability as a percentage and as a decimal.   (4 *marks*)

19 The graph shows the amount of petrol in a car tank during a 500 km journey.

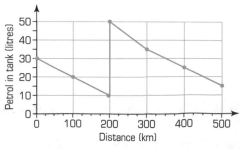

  a How many litres of petrol were in the tank at the start of the journey?
  b How far into the journey was the petrol station?
  c How much petrol was used during the journey in total?   (3 *marks*)

This test is 1 hour long.
You **may** use a calculator for any question in this test.
You will need: pen, pencil, rubber, ruler, protractor, compasses, paper and graph paper.

1 A shop sells video games software.

MOTOR RACING £14·99   GOLF £10·50   FOOTBALL £19·99   SNOOKER £12·00

  a Simon decides to buy the golf and snooker software.
     How much altogether does he pay?
  b The shop offers a special Triple Pack at £34.99.
     You can choose any 3 titles.
     Lara buys Motor Racing, Golf and Football. How much money does
     she save if she buys the Triple Pack?   *(2 marks)*

2 This bar chart shows the number of students that were
absent in 9A last week
  a How many students were absent on Wednesday?
  b Calculate the total number of absences for the whole
     week.
  c On Friday, $\frac{1}{4}$ of the class 9A were absent. Altogether,
     how many students are in the class if they are all present?

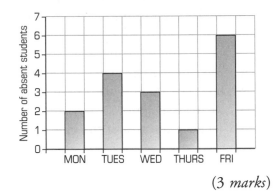

(3 marks)

3 a What number is the arrow pointing to on this scale?

100   200

  b Round this number to the nearest 100.   *(2 marks)*

4 a Write in words the number 139.
  b Write in figures the number ten thousand.   *(2 marks)*

5 a Write the next two numbers in this sequence:

      2, 4, 6, 8, 10, ___, ___

  b What is the special name for these numbers?   *(3 marks)*

6 Here are 4 right-angled triangular tiles
Using all 4 triangles you can make a square as shown.
  a Use all 4 triangles to make a larger right-angled triangle.
     Draw the shape.
  b Use all 4 triangles to make an isosceles trapezium.
     Draw the shape.

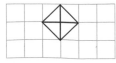

(2 marks)

7 Write the missing numbers in these number chains.

a ⬤18 ▷+36 ⬤ ▷×21.5 ⬤

b ⬤ ▷×11.5 ⬤276

c ⬤36 |+ ▷ ⬤2500

d ⬤ ▷÷0.5 ⬤180

(*5 marks*)

8 Which bottle of shampoo is the better value for money?
Explain your reasoning.

(*2 marks*)

9 The base of this open cube is blue

The open cube is unfolded to give this net:
Write the letter of the square that forms the base.

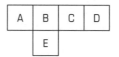

(*1 mark*)

10 a Calculate the perimeter and area of the 'T' shape.
b Draw a rectangle with a perimeter of 10 cm.
Calculate the area.
c Calculate the area of the blue square.

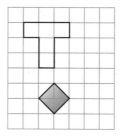

(*5 marks*)

11 The teacher asks two students to think of a number.
Carol chooses the number 4, but Sally chooses a letter *n*.
a Copy and complete the table below.

Teacher's instructions	Carol	Sally
'Think of a number'	4	*n*
'Double the number'	8	
'Add 4 to the answer'	12	
'Subtract 3 from the answer'	9	

b Another student, James, followed the same instructions and got an answer of 15.
What was James' starting number?

(*4 marks*)

12 A school decides to collect tokens from sweet packets.
Eventually 2636 tokens are collected.
The reward scheme is as follows:

Every 25 tokens = £1

The school exchanges as many tokens as it can.
a How much money does the school raise?
b How many tokens are unused and left over?

(*4 marks*)

13 a Using a protractor and ruler, construct this triangle.

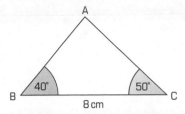

    b Measure   **i**   the angle A
                      ii the length AB
                      iii the length AC.
    c What sort of triangle is ABC?   *(5 marks)*

14 Find the value of the following expressions, when $a = 1$, $b = 3$, $c = 5$:
    a $3c$
    b b^2
    c $a + b + c$
    d abc
    e $5a - b$.   *(5 marks)*

15 You can make these shapes with matches:

shape 1   shape 2   shape 3
4 matches   7 matches   10 matches

The rule to find the number of matches is:

$m = 3s + 1$ where m stands for the number of matches
                    and s stands for the shape number.

    a Use the rule to find how many matches you need for shape 10.
    b Which shape number uses 76 matches?
       Show your working.   *(3 marks)*

16 This flowchart converts pints to millilitres.

    a Change 1 pint to ml.
    b Change 1 litre to pints.   *(2 marks)*

17 Calculate:
    a 35% of 56 kg.
    b $87\frac{1}{2}$% of £46.   *(2 marks)*

18 Draw this cuboid after an enlargement of scale factor 2 on isometric paper.

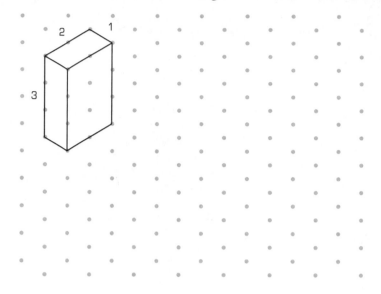

(*1 mark*)

19 The test scores for some students are shown in this bar chart.

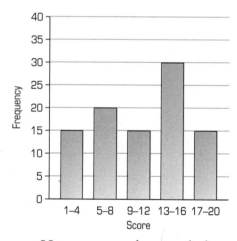

  a How many students took the test?
  b What is the modal group of marks?
  c Jake says 'Someone scored 20 in the test'
     Anna says 'I'm not sure about that. You can't tell from the graph'
     Who is correct? Explain your reasoning.   (*4 marks*)

20 Calculate the unknown angles in these diagrams.

  a   **b**   **c**

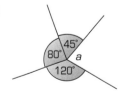   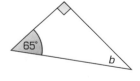   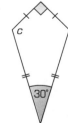

(*3 marks*)

Number

Exercise N1

1 506

2 a 428 **b** 401 **c** 1021

3 a Two-hundred and forty-seven **b** One-thousand three-hundred **c** Nine-hundred and six

4 Eight tenths

5 a 136 **b** 631 **c** 6130

6 a Seven hundreds **b** Seven units **c** Seven tenths

7 a 34 307 **b** 400 006 **c** 85.12

8 a Forty-two thousand, three-hundred and eighty-five **b** Nine-hundred and six-thousand **c** One million

9 a 3.3 **b** 2.9 **c** 3.15

10 a 0 **b** 650 **c** 56 **d** 560 **e** 0.56 **f** 0.056

11 0.45

12 a 3.44 **b** 45.1 **c** 3.61 **d** 4.35 **e** 8 **f** 3.23

13 a 4.23 **b** 0.86 **c** 40

Exercise N2

1 £9

2 a 31 **b** 36 **c** 41 **d** 29

3 a 6, 10, 18, 23, 36 **b** 67, 76, 667, 676, 767 **c** 990, 999, 1000, 1010, 1100

4 24 000

5 a 3.1 **b** 3.8 **c** 4.1 **d** 2.9 **e** 3.25

6 a 2.8, 3, 3.3, 3.8, 3.9 **b** 9, 9.5, 10, 10.1, 10.5 **c** 3.4, 3.46, 3.5, 3.55, 3.6

7 a 3.5 **b** 3.45 **c** 3.05

8 a Potato 3 kg, Carrot 5 kg, Cabbage 56 kg **b** Potato 3.2 kg, Carrot 4.7 kg, Cabbage 56.2 kg

9 a 2468 **b** 8642 **c** 2000, 9000

10 For example, 3.05

11 a < **b** > **c** > **d** > **e** <

12 a 3.62 **b** 3.65 **c** 3.71 **d** 3.59 **e** 3.675

Exercise N3

1 13, 17, or 19 are possible answers

2 a $3 + 7 = 10$ **b** $4 + 6 = 10$

3 a • • • • • • • • • • • • • •   • • • • •   **b** • • • • • • •   7 is prime

4 4-packs, 5   • • • • • •

5 16

6 120

7 a 1, 2, 4, 8, 16, 32 **b** 1, 2, 3, 4, 6, 9, 12, 18, 36

8 a Yes **b** Yes **c** No **d** No

9 g 2, 3, 5, 7, 11, 13, 17, 19, 23, 29, 31, 37, 41, 43, 47, 51, 53, 59, 61, 67, 71, 73, 79, 83, 89, 97

10 a 4 = ∷ **b** 5 = ∷ ⁚ **c** $2n + 2m = 2(n + m); (2n + 1) + (2m + 1) = 2(n + m + 1)$

11 102

12 4 or 9 are possible answers

13 a 8, 16, 24, 32, 40, 48, 56, 64, 72, 80, 88, 96 **b** 6, 12, 18, 24, 30, 36, 42, 48, 54, 60, 66, 72, 78, 84, 90, 96 **c** 24

14 a 1, 2, 4, 5, 10, 20 **b** 1, 2, 5, 10, 25, 50 **c** 10

15 12 minutes

Exercise N4

1 64

2 a 6 **b** ‾5 **c** ‾11

3 ‾6 °C, ‾5 °C, 0 °C, 3 °C, 8 °C

4 a > **b** > **c** > **d** < **e** =

5 4

6 15

7 a 1, 4, 9, 16, 25, 36, 49, 64, 81, 100 **b** 1, 3, 6, 10, 15, 21, 28, 36, 45, 55, 66, 78, 91, 105 **c** 1, 36

8 1

9 a ‾5 °C **b** 16 °C **c** ‾4 °C

10 a = **b** > **c** > **d** >

11 3

12 6

13 a 324 **b** 1 000 000 **c** 7 **d** 30

14

4	‾3	2
‾1	1	3
0	5	‾2

15 a ‾1 **b** $‾4 + ‾3 + ‾1 = ‾8$

Exercise N5

1

2 a 5 **b** $\frac{1}{2}$

3 a i $\frac{1}{3}$ **ii** $\frac{1}{4}$ **iii** $\frac{2}{3}$ **iv** $\frac{1}{2}$ **v** $\frac{1}{4}$ **b i** $\frac{2}{3}$ **ii** $\frac{3}{4}$ **iii** $\frac{1}{3}$ **iv** $\frac{1}{2}$ **v** $\frac{3}{4}$

4 £2.50

5 a $\frac{1}{5}, \frac{2}{5}, \frac{1}{2}, \frac{3}{5}, \frac{4}{5}$ **b**

6 a 16, $\frac{1}{2}$, 36, $\frac{1}{4}$ (from top left to bottom right) **b** 72, $\frac{3}{4}$, $\frac{1}{4}$, $\frac{1}{2}$ (from top left to bottom right)

7 a **b** $\frac{2}{3}$

8 40

9 40

10 a $\frac{3}{4}$ **b** $\frac{7}{8}$ **c** $\frac{3}{4}$ **d** $\frac{8}{9}$

11 a 200 **b** 30

12 a 3 **b** 2 **c** 1

Exercise N6

1 1.5

2

3 a 50% **b** 25% **c** 75%

4 £4

5 £60

6 a 24, 16, 48 (from top right to bottom right, reading from right to left)
b $\frac{1}{2}$, $\frac{1}{4}$, $\frac{3}{4}$ (from top right to bottom right, reading from right to left)

7

8 a 10% **b** 20% **c** 30% **d** 60% **e** 90%

9 200

10 60%

11 0.24, $\frac{1}{4}$, $\frac{13}{50}$, 27%

12 a 30% **b** Car **c** No; 75% of boys walk, but only 60% of girls walk

13 a < **b** > **c** =

Revision R1

1 609

2 a 2 by 9 **b** 7 or 11 or 13 pegs in a row **c** 9 can be 3 by 3

3 two shaded squares

4 12 or 15

5 £10

6 a < **b** = **c** > **d** < **e** > **f** >

7 a 0, 3140 **b** 425, 4250

8 a in order: $\frac{1}{3}, \frac{1}{2}, \frac{5}{6}$. **b** 1, 24, 4

9 24

10 various answers, for example, 120.

11 8

12 a +7 **b** +9, −11

13 £24

14 £4.50, £45, 35%, £5

Exercise N7

1 $\frac{1}{2}$

2 a $\frac{3}{4}$ **b** 0.75 **c** 75%

3 a 4 **b** 15

4 1 : 3

5 9

6 a 45° **b** 135°

7 a 5 : 1 **b** 1 : 10 **c** 1 : 6 **d** 1 : 3 **e** 8 : 1

8 100 g jar. Five of these = 500 g will only cost £12.50 < £13

9 a $\frac{3}{4}$ **b** 75%

10 60p

11 a 2 : 3 **b** 3 : 4 **c** 2 : 3 **d** 3 : 5 **e** 5 : 8

12 150 ml of milk, 6 eggs

13 Danny gets £40, Benny gets £60

Exercise N8

1 Yes

2 a 527 **b** 648

3 a 748 **b** 665 **c** 19 **d** 21 **e** 21

4 a T **b** F **c** T **d** F

5 £16

6 a 30 **b** 15

7 a £5 **b** £10

8 a $3 + 5 = 10 - 2$ **b** $12 \div 3 = 10 - 6$ **c** $4 \div 4 = 5 - 4$ **d** $3 \times 3 = 18 \div 2$

9 a $(3 + 4 + 2) \times 3 + 27$ **b** $3 + ((4 + 2) \times 3) = 21$

10 $15 \times 3 = 45$

11 100

12

x	2	4	6
3	6	12	18
5	10	20	30
7	14	28	42

13 a 8 **b** 3.375

14 $15 \times 55 = 825$

Exercise N9

1 8 **2** 84 **3** 56 **4** 36 **5** 6 **6** 45

7 250 **8** £25 **9** 6 **10** 101 **11** 42 **12** 15

13 89% **14** 45p **15** 44 **16** 164 **17** 91 **18** $x = 5$

19 40 **20** 144 cm^2 **21** 14 **22** 204 **23** 400 **24** 25

25 10 **26** 8.64

Exercise N10

1 398 mm **2 a** 83 **b** 68 **3 a** £13.37 **b** £6.63

4 562 **5** 366 **6** 18 **7** 39

8 a 3701 **b** 633 **9** 9221 **10** 183 **11** 19.98

12 a 13.23 **b** 6.89 **13 a** 12.01 m **b** 4.85 m **14** 0.06 m **15** 2.9

16 5.3 **17** 4.6 **18 a** 11.6 **b** 8.1 **c** 11.6

Exercise N11

1 a 230 **b** 34 **2** £6.25 **3** 216 **4** 51

5 a 4 **b** 2 **6** 468 **7** 123 **8 a** 576 **b** 736

9 £6.75 **10** 504 **11** 32p **12 a** 58.2 **b** 60.9

13 a 0.9 **b** 1.05 **14** £14.25 **15** £200 cash is cheaper, by £10

16 £75.60 **17** 21.08 cm^2 **18 a** £14 **b** £12.50 **c** 52-week is better value

19 1.76 **20 a** 9.6 m **b** £23.04

Exercise N12

1 £15.30 **2** £65.80

3 a 13.1 **b** 3.15 **4 a** £268.70 **b** Total is £18.70 more than £250

5 a £3.25 **b** £3.45 **c** £4.20 **6 a** 23 **b** 35

7 a 24.5 **b** 17.5 **c** 6 **d** 73.5 **8 a** 4.24 (2 dp) **b** 4.47 (2 dp) **c** 7.75 (2 dp)

9 a 44.8 **b** 3 **10** £2.40

11 4.08 **12 a** £2.52 **b** £6.37

13 8 full glasses, 200 ml left in bottle **14** 12

Revision R2

1 5 **2** 110

3 a 60 **b** 5, 6, 10 **4 a** 573 **b** 446 **c** 168 **d** 26

5 a 120 **b** £11.60 **c** £2.90 **d** 5 **6** 75p

7 a 325, 6, 780, 1300 **b** 1040 **8 a** 18, 10 **b** 60 **c** $(4 + 5 + 1) \times 5$ **d** $4 + (5 + 1) \times 5$

9 5.25 **10** 1725, 569

11 1.2 kg **12 a** 58 **b** £24 360 **c** £8.12

13 a 600 ml **b** 50 ml **c** no, 1 out of 5 is 20% **14** 28

15 20 **16 a** £33.25 **b** 14

Algebra

Exercise A1

1 12

2 10

3 **a** 7 **b** 16 **c** 13 **d** 2 **e** 16

4 **a** 2 **b** 47 **c** ⁻3

5 **a** $4n$ **b** $4n$ **c** $6n$

6 **a** 12 cm **b** 12 cm **c** 20 cm **d** 11 cm **e** 18 cm

7 **a** $2x+8$ **b** $3x+6$ **c** $8x+80$

8 This is true if and only if you are a 14 year old, as $2 \times 1 \times 7 = 14$

9 **a** $8+y$ **b** y

10 $5(4+2) = 5 \times 6 = 30$, $5 \times 4 + 10 = 20 + 10 = 30$.

11 $4a+2b$

12 Kieren, as $6 \times 4 = 24$

13 $d=3$

14 **a** $5t+3$ **b** $9d+3$ **c** 0

15 $a+2b+c$

Exercise A2

1 3

2 3

3 **a** $a=10$ **b** $b=6$ **c** $c=4$

4 $A=ab$

5 **a** 5 minutes **b** $(n+2)$ minutes

6 **a** $x=8$ **b** $y=3$

7 5 miles

8 **a** $3n$ **b** $3n+5$

9 $n-2$

10 $b=30$

11 **a** 212 °F **b** 32 °F **c** 68 °F

12 $W=Ph$

13 **a** $x=12$ **b** $x=13$

14 **a** T **b** T **c** F

15 $180 = 90 + 2a \rightarrow a = 45°$

Exercise A3

1 50

2 **a** 500, 600, 700 **b** 0, 25, 125

3 25

4 **a**

b 13, 17 **c** Number of dots in nth pattern is $4(n-1)+1$. Hence number of dots in tenth pattern is 37

5 **a** 21, 28 **b** Triangular numbers **c**

6 **a**

b 3, 5, 7, 9 **c** Number of matchsticks in the nth pattern is $3+2n$. Number of matchsticks in the 10th pattern is 23

7 **a** 8, 13, 18, 23, 28 **b** 53

8 **a** 1, 10, 100, 1000, 10000 **b** Yes, it is the 7th term

9 13, 19

10 **a**

Pattern number	1	2	3	4	5
Term	1	3	5	7	9

b 19

11 **a** 36 **b**

Exercise A4

1 9

2 **a** 3 **b** 6 **c** 9 **d** 12 **e** 15

3 13

4 **a** 12 **b** Each arrow goes from n to $2n$, for $1 \leqslant 12$

5 **a** ⁻2 **b** 2 **c** 6 **d** 10 **e** 14

6 **a** 8 **b** 3 **c** Add 4 **d** Subtract 8

7 $n \rightarrow n-4$

8 a 1, 5, 7 **b**

9 $y = 2x$

10 a

x	y	Coordinates
0	3	(0, 3)
1	4	(1, 4)
2	5	(2, 5)
3	6	(3, 6)

b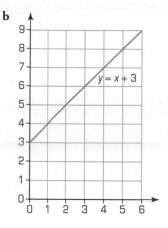

Exercise A5

1 a £20 **b** £60

2 a 50 °F **b** 95 °F **c** 21 °C **d** 5 °C **e** 99 °F

3 a 20p **b** 120p **c** 4 packets **d** 7 packets **e** 200p

4 a £12 **b** 2 miles **c**

Miles	1	2	3	4	5	6	7	8	9	10
Cost (£)	6	7	8	9	10	11	12	13	14	15

e 5 miles

d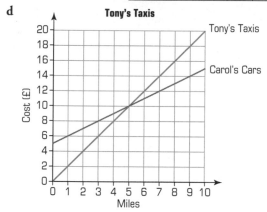

Revision R3

1 a 50 **b** 80, 100, 120 **c** ⁻10, 0, 10 **d** ⁻3, 13; 4

2 a $p = 3a$ **b** $p = 3b + 2c$ **c** $p = 2d + 7$ **d** $p = 4e + 4f + 8$

3 a add 12; multiply by 3; multiply by 2 then add 6 **b** halve it

4 13

5 a 77 °F, 80 °F **b** 32 °F, 30 °F **c** 50 °F, 50 °F

6 a 1 and 5, 2 and 4, 3 and 3, 4 and 2, 5 and 1 **b** points at (1, 1) (2, 2) (3, 3) (4, 4) (5, 5) and (6, 6)
c one less than the red dice

7 a 48, 72 **b** points at (0, 0) (10, 24) (20, 48) (30, 72) **c** 50, 64 **d** points at (0, 22) (10, 36) (20, 50) and (30, 64) **e** 22

8 a $7 + 5t$ **b** $3b + 17$

9 40

10 $n + 5$

Shape

Exercise S1

1 Equilateral triangle

2 90°

3 a **b** **c** **d**

4 a 360° **b** 180° **c** 90°

5 180°

6 a 144° **b** 26° **c** 236° **d** 136° **e** 42° **f** 80°

7 a and b

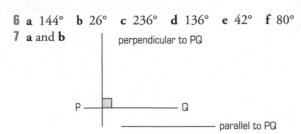

8 a 8 cm **b** 68° **c** 44° **d** Isosceles

9 50°

10 a 72°, the triangle is isosceles **b** 46°, the angles on a straight line add up to 180° **c** 60°, the triangle is equilateral

d $d = 135°$, as the angles on a straight line add up to 180°; $e = 25°$, as the angles in a triangle add up to 180°

e 120°, as the angle in a circle is 360°

f $f = 37°$, as opposite angles are equal; $g = h = 143°$, as opposite angles are equal, and the angle in a circle is 360°

Exercise S2

1 90°

2 a 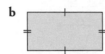 **b** 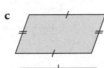 **c** **d** no parallel lines.

3 a 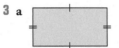 **b** **c**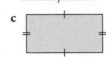

4 360°

5 a **b** Isosceles trapezium

6 a **b**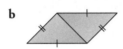

7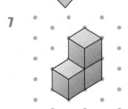

8 70°

9 Rhombus

10

11 B

Exercise S3

1 Rectangle

2 a 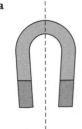 **b** No lines of symmetry **c**  **d**  **3**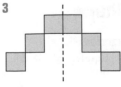

4 3

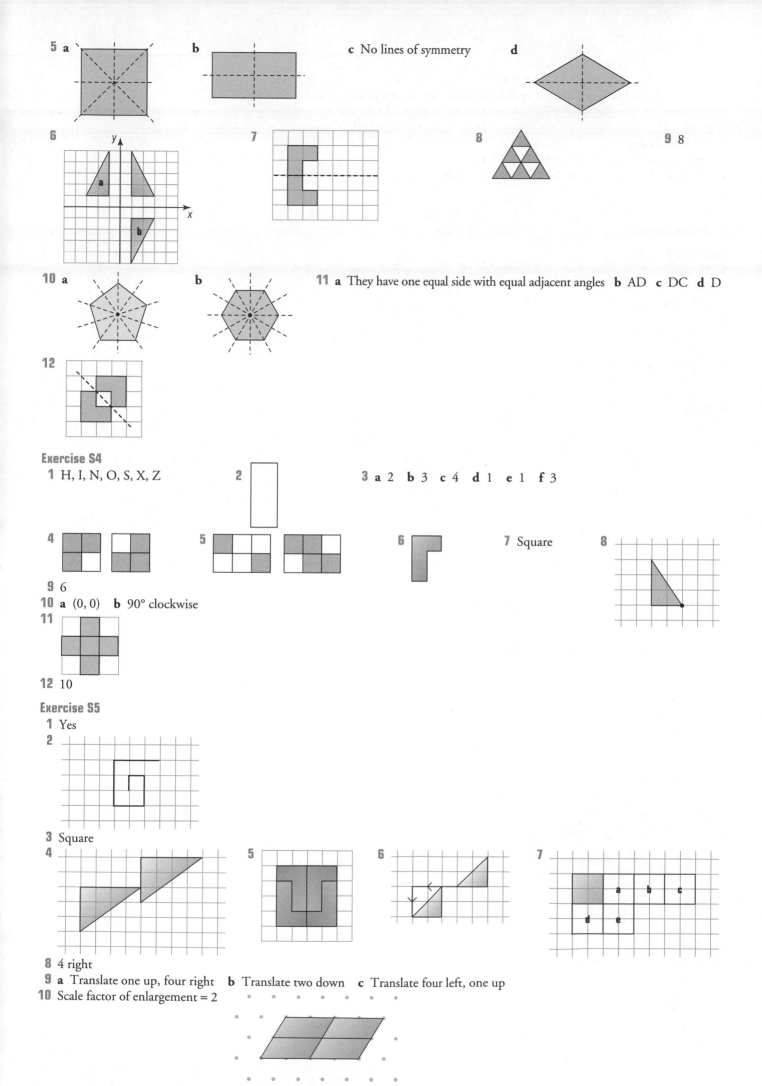

5 a   **b**   **c** No lines of symmetry   **d**

6   **7**   **8**   **9** 8

10 a   **b**   **11 a** They have one equal side with equal adjacent angles   **b** AD   **c** DC   **d** D

12

Exercise S4

1 H, I, N, O, S, X, Z

2

3 a 2   **b** 3   **c** 4   **d** 1   **e** 1   **f** 3

4   **5**   **6**   **7** Square   **8**

9 6

10 a (0, 0)   **b** 90° clockwise

11

12 10

Exercise S5

1 Yes

2

3 Square

4   **5**   **6**   **7**

8 4 right

9 a Translate one up, four right   **b** Translate two down   **c** Translate four left, one up

10 Scale factor of enlargement = 2

Exercise S6

1 (2, 4)

2 a (⁻2, 1) **b** (2, 2) **c** (0, 1) **d** (0, 2)

3 a (8, 4) **b** (20, 10), you double the y-coordinate. **c** No, $2 \times 12 = 24$ so the point is (24, 12).

4 (2, 2)

5 (4, 2)

6 (3, 1), (3, 2) or (3, 4)

7 Any point with y-coordinate 0: (1, 0) (2, 0) etc.

8 a square **b** parallelogram **c** kite **d** trapezium **e** arrowhead

Exercise S7

1 90°   **2 a** 5 cm, 2.2 cm **b** 50 mm, 22 mm   **3 a** 30° **b** 150°   **4** 330°

5–9 Constructions

Exercise S8

1 25   **2 a** 70 cm **b**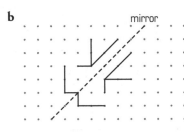

3 17 kg

4 100.9 cm

5 4.8 °C

6 a 4 pm **b** 10 am **c** 6 pm

7 9 pm

8 a 1.5 kg **b** 35 °C **c** 240 ml

9 a 59 °F **b** 10.5 °C

Revision R4

1 a 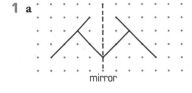 **b**   **c**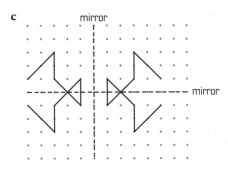

2 none

3 a E **b** D **c** B

4 a 90° **b** 6 **c** 30° **d** 150° **e** 60 minutes

5 a A and D **b** (5, 7) **c** (7, 5) **d** (7, 1)

6 square

7 a (6, y), $y \neq 6$ **b** (8, 5) or (8, ⁻3) or (4, 5) or (4, ⁻3)

8

		lines		
		0	1	2	3
order	1	E	F		
	2	B		C	
	3	D			A

9 a cone **b** accurate construction

10 accurate construction

11 a 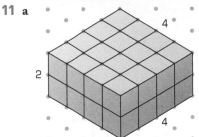 **b** 24 cubes

Exercise S9

1 a 3 m **b** 30 cm **c** 4 m **d** 60 km **e** 30 mm

2 a km **b** cm **c** m

3 a 1 cm **b** 10 cm **c** 100 cm **d** 150 cm **e** 105 cm

4 a 1600 m **b** 1.6 km

5 10 mm

6 Kelly (147 cm), Brett (148 cm), Jason (150 cm)

7 30 cm

8 16 km

9 More

10 $3\frac{1}{3}$ feet

11 400 miles

Exercise S10

1 1 kg

3 500 ml

5 2.5 kg

7 No, as 3 × 330 ml = 990 ml < 1000 ml = 1 litre

9 a 1000 ml **b** 2500 ml **c** 10 ml **d** 100 ml **e** 1000 ml

11 600 ml

13 4

2 10 l

4 a kg **b** ml

6 a 2.2 pounds **b** 5 kg

8 a 500 g **b** 0.5 kg

10 8

12 More

14 Less

Exercise S11

1 a 5 square units **b** 5 square units **c** 7 square units **d** 7 square units **e** 6 square units

2 a 12 units **b** 12 units **c** 16 units **d** 16 units **e** 14 units

3 64 cm²

4 a 4 **b** 8 **c** 15 **d** 12 **e** 36

5

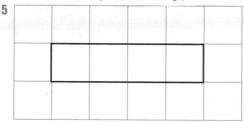

6 a 24 cm² **b** 3 cm²

7 20.8 cm

8 30 cm²

9 9 cm²

10 a 16 square units **b** 14 square units **c** 24 square units **d** 32 square units **e** 66 square units

11 a 10 cm² **b** 36 cm²

Data

Exercise D1

1 a 30 **b** 3 **c** 25

2 a 11 **b** August **c** Ardèche

3 a Top labels: Yes/No, Side labels: Boys/Girls **b**

Number of absences	Tally	Frequency
0–2	IIII IIII IIII IIII	19
3–5	IIII	4
6–8		0
9+	I	1

4 a The categories 'sometimes' and 'occasionally' are too similar. They are ambiguous

b Daily/Every other day/Once a week **c** 'Five of her friends' is too small a sample size to be able to draw any conclusions

5 B. It is easier to fill in as people answer questions

6 a The categories overlap e.g. '0–10', '10–20'. **b**

Mark	Tally	Frequency
0–9		
10–19		
20–29		
30–39		
40–50		

Exercise D2

1 a 4 and 7 **b** 4

2 Jack and Emily were the most popular names for baby boys and girl, respectively, born in 2003

3 65%

4 5

5 a 5 **b** 6

6 150–159 cm

7 a 7 and 8 **b** 8 **c** 5.4 **d** 6

8 a 41 **b** No. The average is slightly higher than 40

9 3, 4, 5

10 4, 5, 6

11 a 35 **b** 6

Revision R5

1 a 30 **b** 23 **c** 12, 12 **d** 4, 3 **e** 10, 13
                            5, 3   1, 2   4, 4

2 a 2 litres **b** 2 m **c** 100 g

3 11 am

4 a

4	ЖЖ	5
5	ЖЖ I	6
6	ЖЖ	5
7	ЖЖ III	8
8	III	3
9	II	2

b 7 **c** 13 trainers are bigger than 6 and 18 other sized trainers were sold

5 100

6 a 30 **b** 24

7 mass or weight

8 mean is 39.9 km

9 a 6 **b** 2

10 a 14 oz **b** 225 g–235 g **c** 34 oz–36 oz

11 a 3 by 4, 4 by 3, 6 by 2 **b** 40 cm

Exercise D3

1
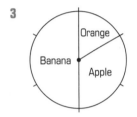

2
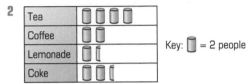

3
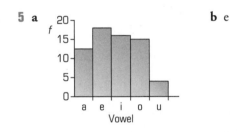

4 a
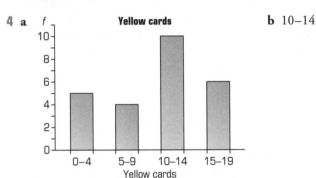
b 10–14

5 a
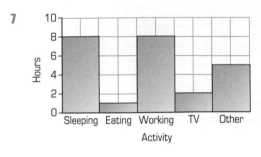
b e

6
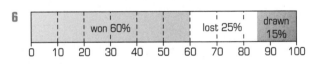

7
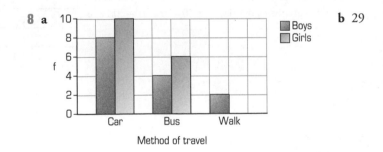

8 a

b 29

Exercise D4

1 a The Court **b** 15 **c** 70

2 a 2 items **b** 10 **c** 7

3 25 people

4 a 50° **b** 9 **c** You would expect each number to come up an equal number of times, but 1 comes up more than any other number, so the dice could be biased.

5 a 23 mm **b** Thursday

6 75%

7 a 60% **b** 45 female, 30 male

8 32 students

Exercise D5

1 9

2 a Internet **b** Chat room **c** 9 **d** 27

3 a 2 **b** 12 **c** $\frac{1}{3}$

4 35%

5 9

6 a 12–19 **b** The grouping '12–19' does not tell you the youngest person questioned; similarly the grouping '60–69' does not tell you the oldest – so you cannot find the difference (the range) of these two (unknown) numbers either.

7 a 30% **b i** 4 **ii** 6 **iii** 6 **iv** 4

Exercise D6

1 7

2 a Maths **b** 5 **c** He is incorrect – 10 boys like maths, but only 5 girls do

3 a 900 m **b** 1160 m **c** People walk less on average today than fifteen years ago

4 a 2, 3, 3, 5, 7, 8, 8, 8, 9, 10 **b** Mean = 6.3, Range = 8 **c** 3, 4, 5, 5, 5, 7, 8 **d** Mean = 5.625, Range = 5
   e On average the girls did better in the test **f** The range of abilities is greater in the girls; boys show less variation in ability

5 a 1700 hrs **b** April

Exercise D7

1 0

2 a Blue **b** Black and White, as there are two balls each of these colours

3 a It will be windy every day for a month/Unlikely
   A baby girl will be born somewhere in the world tomorrow/Certain
   A man will walk on Jupiter tomorrow/Impossible
   It will be sunny sometime in the next week/Likely

b

4 0.1

5 a 0.5 **b** 0.5 **c** 0.5 **d** 0.5

6 250

7 a $\frac{7}{10}$ **b** 30 **c** 70

8 a

b 3

Exercise D8

1 P(card is lower) = $\frac{1}{2}$ > $\frac{4}{10}$ = P(card is higher), so the second card is more likely to be lower

2 $\frac{1}{2}$

3 $\frac{3}{5}$

4 a $\frac{1}{11}$ **b** $\frac{2}{11}$ **c** $\frac{4}{11}$ **d** $\frac{7}{11}$

5 PP, PB, PK, BP, BB, BK, KP, KB, KK

6 a

	1	2	3	4	5	6
1	2	3	4	5	6	7
2	3	4	5	6	7	8
3	4	5	6	7	8	9
4	5	6	7	8	9	10
5	6	7	8	9	10	11
6	7	8	9	10	11	12

b 7 **c** 36 **d** $\frac{1}{18}$ **e** $\frac{7}{36}$ **f** $\frac{5}{18}$

7 $\frac{1}{4}$

8 Louis, as you would need to count how many counters of each colour there were to find the probability.

9

Flavour	Probability	Number of cartons
Vanilla	$\frac{1}{2}$	6
Cherry	$\frac{1}{3}$	4
Raspberry	$\frac{1}{6}$	2

Revision R6

1 Male ⬤⬤   Female ⬤◖

2 a △ , ⬤, ◼   **b** ◼; there are more of them   **c** circles   **d** ⬤⬤ and ◼

3 1, 3, 5, 7, 9

4 a Liz   **b** Jim   **c** Gives a good idea of the overall winner.   **d** Gives specific detail about each game.

5 $\frac{5}{8}$

6 a about 20%   **b** about 37%   **c** about 40 000
   d Generally female teachers tend to be younger. 20–29 and 30–39 bars are larger for female teachers

7 a Les Tom, Nia Tom, Ann Tom   **b** $\frac{7}{8}$

8 a September   **b** May, June, Oct, Nov, Dec   **c** Jan, Feb, Dec

Practice Test Paper 1 (non-calculator)   Tier 3–5

1 a 12   **b** 10   **c** 4 (3)

2 a 741   **b** 262   **c** 224   **d** 49 (4)

3 $1 \times 1 \times 24, 1 \times 2 \times 12, 1 \times 4 \times 6, 2 \times 3 \times 4$ (2)

4 a 6 pieces   **b** 3 pieces   **c** 3 pieces (4)

5 a 80   **b** 120 (3)

6 a , b   **c** 21 °C (3)

7 a right angled, isosceles   **b** (4, 6)   **c** (4, 0) (4)

8 2.5 m (2)

9 a obtuse   **b** 130°   **c** your own angle of 48°. (3)

10 4 glasses (2)

11 A: $4a$, B: $3a$ (2)

12 a 23, 19   **b** $4 \times (5 + 3) = 32$ (3)

13 a A and C   **b** your own triangle. (4)

14 a £6   **b** £20   **c** £10.50 (6)

15 a £70.20   **b** £1.75 (4)

16 a $k = 2$ **b** $m = 4\frac{1}{2}$ (2)

17 3, 4 and 6 OR 2, 4 and 5 (2)

18 a $\frac{3}{5}$ **b** at $\frac{6}{10}$ **c** 60%, 0.6 (4)

19 a 30 l   **b** 200 km   **c** 55 l (3)

Practice Test Paper 2 (calculator)   Tier 3–5

1 a £22.50   **b** £10.49 (2)

2 a 3   **b** 16   **c** 24 (3)

3 a 160   **b** 200 (2)

4 a One hundred and thirty nine   **b** 10 000 (2)

5 a 12, 14   **b** even numbers (3)

6 a   **b**   (2)

7 a 54, 1161   **b** 24   **c** 2464   **d** 90 (5)

8 250 ml or £1.80, $2 \times 250 = 500$ ml, $2 \times £1.80 = £3.60$ (2)

9 E (1)

10 a 12 cm, 5 cm^2 **b** either 3 by 2 or 4 by 1 rectangles with areas 6 cm^2 and 4 cm^2 respectively   **c** 2 cm^2 (5)

11 a $2n, 2n + 1$ **b** 7 (4)

12 a £105   **b** 11 unused tokens (4)

13 a your own construction   **b** 90°, AB = 6.1 cm, AC = 5.1 cm   **c** right-angled $\angle$ scalene (5)

14 a 3   **b** 9   **c** 9   **d** 15   **e** 2 (5)

15 a 31   **b** Shape 25, $3s + 1 = 76$, $3s = 75$, $s = 25$ (3)

16 a 568 ml   **b** 1.76 pints (2)

17 a 19.6 kg   **b** £40.25 (2)

18 cuboid measuring 2 by 4 by 6 (1)

19 a 95 students   **b** 13–16   **c** Anna, 15 students got marks in the 17–20 range, but we don't know the actual marks. (4)

20 a 115°   **b** 25°   **c** 120° (3)